FROM SQUARE ONE

A Meditation, with Digressions, on Crosswords

Dean Olsher

Scribner

New York   London   Toronto   Sydney

FROM SQUARE ONE

Magnificent Obsession

There is no other word for it. I get defensive when people dismiss the crossword as a mere pastime or, worse, a form of escapism. To my mind, they just don't get it.

Alfred Hitchcock didn't get it. He told François Truffaut, "I don't really approve of whodunits because they're rather like a jigsaw or a crossword puzzle. No emotion. You simply wait to find out who committed the murder."

Here, Hitchcock fell prey to a false dichotomy, and it's a common one: that thinking and feeling are an either/or proposition. In fact they are inextricable. Encountering a powerful idea can be a deeply moving experience. Anyone who believes that cerebral and emotional satisfaction are at odds with each other need only open any book by Vladimir Nabokov, who, as it happens, created the world's first known Russian-language crossword puzzles while exiled in Berlin during the 1920s.

Perhaps Hitchcock saw only suspense, terror, and imminent jeopardy as emotions. It is true that you will find none of these states of being in the crossword, unless you count yourself among the throngs who have decided they can't solve puzzles and are therefore scared to death of them.

Exhilaration is an emotion. So is serenity. For those native to the world of the puzzle, entering a crossword is like stepping into the clean white cube of an art gallery or into a church or a Japanese rock garden. There are days when solving puzzles feels like a practice, the next best thing to seated meditation. When beautifully executed, a crossword can bring about the same response as a work of art.

It is more honest, though, to think of crosswords as a habit, like smoking. It's just something to do, every day, because it's there. When finished with a puzzle, I don't pump my fists in triumph or congratulate myself for my perseverance. I solve crosswords because they bring on a feeling of emptiness, and paradoxically, that feeling seems to fill a hole deep inside. It's not a release, it's not a flushing out, although both those terms grasp at some aspect of it. Norman Mailer said that for him, solving the crossword every day was like combing his brain. This simile is strong because it has nothing to do with mental fitness. It's not about intelligence or holding on to memory. Crosswords bring about a focused state of mind, the elusive "flow state."

Then there are days when I decide that this is all an elaborate self-deception. That the puzzle is indeed an escape mechanism. That crossword addiction is not a metaphor but a destructive, literal truth.

The Geography of Puzzle-Land

Time ruins everything. Because of it, food spoils, breasts sag, loved ones die. As a species we have developed clever ways to try to stop it—by looking at paintings and photographs, or even sometimes through the supremely temporal art form of music. Bill Evans playing "Detour Ahead" convinces you that you have, for the moment, stepped out of time.

The crossword eliminates time. It is a daily dip of the toe into the world conjured for Billy Pilgrim by Kurt Vonnegut, himself a lover of crosswords. True, Billy was shell-shocked and probably crazy even before he lived through the firebombing of Dresden. Still, I am convinced that we solve crosswords to become unstuck in time.

When immersed in the grid, the Emancipation Proclamation rubs elbows with HAL 9000. Thoughts bounce from the birthright of ESAU (convention dictates that crossword answers be rendered in all capital letters) to that Sunday afternoon thirty years ago when my mother, on the couch, awed by a particularly clever piece of crossword misdirection, exclaimed, "What an amazing language," prompting me to wonder, *Is that true? More amazing than the others?* If we tire of the GALAPAGOS Islands, we can skip over to EMO music in no time flat. While we may not be omniscient, it is the closest we can come to approaching omnipresence.

A recent theory for why we dream: our brain is playing Tetris. Whether we are sleeping in our beds or sleepwalking in front of this powerfully addictive video game, the mind needs to fit the scattered bits of our day together and file them accordingly. Stare at the black squares of a puzzle long enough and you will notice the same Lego-like shapes that fall from the Tetris sky. The crossword creates a similar opportunity to find linkages between the apparently unrelated experiences of our lives.

In 1884, Edwin Abbott conceived of a world stripped of the third dimension and named it Flatland. Crossword puzzles exist outside the dimension of time, too, in the place the logician Raymond Smullyan named Puzzle-Land. Having an experience there is more spatial than temporal. In starting a puzzle, we step off the freeway of our lives on which we speed inexorably toward death, and enter into a place of stasis.

Do puzzles provide the only route to this place? Of course not. We pursue all kinds of endeavors—sex, drugs, yoga—to get there. Seeing things this way should not diminish our interest in puzzles but stoke it. It gives us an incentive to construct a natural history of the crossword. Examining its anatomy is the only way to understand its parasitic relationship to its host, the human organism.

The Tyranny of Narrative

The crossword is a pageant of people, places, and things—not as they are but the *ideas* of them, as they might appear in Plato's cave. In this world, any unanswered questions of real life melt away. URI Geller is simply a "mentalist" or "spoon bender." Here his main value is the attractive arrangement of vowels and consonants in his name. Besides, it has never been clear why one would want spoons bent in the first place.

In the world of the crossword, we are freed from the straitjacket of narrative linearity, which is one-dimensional, and get to stretch our legs in two dimensions and more. Cinema has been trying to do the same over the last few decades, following in the footsteps of the French *nouveau roman* by reordering the chronology. Still, those stories reorganize themselves after the fact into a series of events with a beginning, middle, and end. Like the phone book, the crossword boasts a rich cast of characters and no plot.

There are so many nonnarrative ways to engage the mind, and still our culture puts stories front and center.

We are drowning in stories, whereas poetry subsists in the margins. It is no coincidence that one of America's most popular poets, Billy Collins, is essentially a prose writer who adds extra line breaks. Meanwhile, "storytelling" is uttered with the same reverence that politicians reserve for "family." How long before we are all sick to death of hearing other people's tales, as if each and every one of them were sacred? Joseph Campbell explained once and for all that there are not, in fact, eight million stories in the naked city but rather the same story eight million times. Enough with the stories.

The impulse to explain—in other words, journalism—is epidemic. Artists are now expected, in interviews and DVD commentaries, to give exegeses of their work instead of letting it speak for itself. The crossword offers daily relief from story, explanation, journalism. It engages the mind as a work of poetry, the parallelism of its themed entries serving the role of rhyme. A puzzle is not *about* anything. It is just an experience, with an arbitrary beginning, middle, and end that are unique for each solver. It's an accumulation of facts, like a *New Yorker* article from the Harold Ross years. We enjoy bursts of insight as we hopscotch over islands of meaning, and then it's over.

And so it goes with this book. What follows is a kind of diary, or journal, but with a crucial difference, since those concepts, derived as they are from words for *day*, are themselves bound up in the notion of time. The entries here carry no time stamp. They are instead a collection of dispatches from Puzzle-Land, stopping for a time at Alice's rabbit hole and meeting the occasional quirky word nerd but more often people who, for better or worse, use crosswords as a vital coping mechanism—

for loneliness, depression, obsessiveness. Along the way, things will happen, to be sure, but the goal is less to recount a series of incidents (narrative, linear, one-dimensional) than it is to jump around the outline of this timeless, two-dimensional mental space—a latticework of associations going across and down—that is suggested by the crossword puzzle. And when we're done, instead of arriving at the end of a road, we will look down on the space we have delineated, as if from a satellite above Earth.

The Making of a Crossword

"Did you wear a tie for the occasion?" I asked Francis Heaney soon after I arrived at his home in Brooklyn.

"I wear ties for *every* occasion."

This I knew to be true, as well as the fact that Francis spends a good deal of time finding shirts and ties with wild patterns and colors that seem as if they were conceived together for some kind of costume, even though they were bought separately. The goal for this visit was the construction of a crossword puzzle. I had come to watch Francis make one from the beginning.

What first drew my attention to the special way Francis's mind works was his cartoon, "Six Things," published in his blog, Heaneyland! Its puzzlelike construction helped clarify for me what is so appealing about crosswords—or a well-made piece of radio, or art in general, for that matter. "Six Things" is a textbook example of the joys that ensue when a creator trusts his or her audience and allows the last part to come together in the end user's brain.

The conceit is simple. In each installment of "Six Things," Francis writes a title and then illustrates it with six pictures and captions in his rudimentary, Thurberesque style. Take, for example, "Twelfths":

Six Things. Or Half a Thing, Depending on How You Look at It.

Resisting the didactic, the explanatory, and the journalistic, Francis instead hands out a few leaves of romaine, an heirloom tomato, and some finely shaved pecorino and says, "Here, make the salad yourself."

Francis welcomed me in. His wife, Rose, was in San Francisco, visiting her boyfriend (they are polyamorous), but her presence was evident in the form of a spinning wheel she uses to make yarn. You might argue that, as busywork goes, knitting is slightly more useful than crosswords. I would disagree.

As Francis led me toward his workspace he mentioned he

had spent the previous two hours cleaning up for my arrival, although, he added, that might not be evident. I agreed in silence, looking around for the cat that I had not yet seen but could detect nonetheless. The environment reinforced an observation once passed on by a musicologist, who explained that chaotic societies tend to give rise to highly organized art. Think of Motown, or bel canto opera. This is how it works.

Snapshots

The woman in the wheelchair, staring toward a fourth-floor apartment on University Place, her mouth AGAPE. Her helper, crouched next to her, pencil in one hand and crossword in the other, waiting for a blink to signal what to fill in next.

The pretty girl on the subway, immersed in a grid. For some, this is an invitation to stick a toe into a door that seems AJAR. I see it otherwise: the crossword is a universal symbol for Stay Away from Me.

The Greenwich Village café. Inside, *Village Voice* food writer Robert Sietsema, solving the *New York Times* crossword with his daughter when she is home from college. It's not clear what is more appealing: the closeness between parent and child, or the simple fact of the crossword uniting two people instead of pushing them apart.

Fifty Million Americans Can't Be Wrong

The statistic is repeated often, particularly in book-jacket blurbs. The one about 50 million Americans solving crossword puzzles on a regular basis.

The skeptic within asks: How do you know?

The reply, from more than one person, is: Ask Stanley Newman.

Before he became editor of the *Newsday* crossword, Newman had several careers, one of which involved market research. Fifty million is actually on the conservative side of a range he came up with—50 to 60 million—using data provided by the Newspaper Advertising Bureau, which used to commission regular readership surveys. Its research showed that 25 to 30 percent of newspaper readers solved crosswords "at least occasionally." That means that at the time of Newman's inquiry, there were around 200 million newspaper readers.

Newman's numbers, however, are no longer reliable. We know, for example, that readership has dropped sharply since 1990, and even more since the rise of the Internet. Did these declines bring with them a drop in crossword solving, too? The Newspaper Advertising Bureau is of no help. It stopped commissioning readership surveys when it ceased to exist as such in 1992 and was folded into the Newspaper Association of America. My attempts to get data from them resulted in contradictory responses, the first being that they don't seek such information, the second being that they don't reveal such information, and the third being a telephonic slam of the door in my ear.

Besides. 50 million? That seemed suspiciously high.

And so I commissioned a poll. You might be surprised to find out how easy it was to do. I just found the names of several reputable pollsters and picked the least expensive. For $750, Wayne Russum of the Opinion Research Corporation arranged for his team of phone callers to ask one thousand people the following multipart question: "How often do you do crossword puzzles in the newspaper? A few times a week or more often? Once a week or less often? Never?"

Then, to go Stanley Newman one step further, I requested a demographic breakdown. After all, it's not enough to know how many Americans do crosswords. We want to know how old they are. Do they live alone? Are there more of them in cities or in rural areas?

The newspaper itself provides the beginning of an answer to this question on a daily basis. It's how we know that Barbara M. Parks, a knitter, did crossword puzzles and kept in touch with her many friends; that Helen Petrauskas, from Michigan, who helped introduce air bags as standard equipment in cars, enjoyed a large garden and reading history, physics, and British mysteries, and also indulged in difficult crossword puzzles; and that Lillian Paul of Helena, Minnesota, enjoyed knitting, doing crossword puzzles, and working in her rose garden before she went home to the Lord.

In my mind, the quintessential crossword lover is an aging woman at the breakfast nook using the puzzle as an invisible shield that provides at least a few blessed minutes of protection from her husband.

But the obituary pages give an incomplete picture.

As nice as it would have been to use this poll to round out the profile, each additional question would have doubled, then tripled the invoice. I settled for finding out the respondents' gender, age, education, geographic location by region, and household income.

The report arrived. I waited several minutes to open it. It was an important moment. After all, I finally possessed hard data that promised to give definitive answers. How many people *really* solve puzzles? What are they like?

The report consisted of pages and pages of tables and numbers in small print. I had no idea what they meant.

I asked Kathy Frankovic, who has since retired from her longtime job as Director of Surveys for CBS News, to interpret the data. First, I wanted her to give me an idea of the prototypical crossword solver. She looked over the numbers and declared there is no such thing.

As it happens, slightly more men than women do crosswords, but the difference is statistically insignificant. The distribution seems to be weighted a little toward southern "metro" areas, but Frankovic explained that is a meaningless term. There's a small bulge in the column for the 65+ age group, but a sizeable chunk in the 35–44 group, too. The crossword appeals to adults of all ages. If my $750 revealed anything, it's the not very newsworthy datum that crossword puzzlers are likely to be college graduates with an income above $75,000.

Now, about that 50 million.

Remember Newman's oft-repeated claim is that 50 million Americans do crossword puzzles "at least occasionally." The way I phrased the question, with a great deal of help from Wayne Russum, was: How many adult Americans do crosswords once a week or less often? The answer, according to the Opinion Research Corporation, is 29 percent.

This next part is so easy to do even I can manage it all by myself. The U.S. Census Bureau reports that the population of adults 18 years and older in 2004 was 220,377,000. Multiply that number by .29 and you get 63,909,330.

Turns out Newman's figure was practically dead-on, and even on the slightly conservative side. To be sure, I would have been happier if my $750 overturned some misguided paradigm. But certainty is its own reward. It is always better to know a thing than not to know it.

Even Ken Jennings Thinks So, and He Knows a Lot of Things

Jeopardy! champion Ken Jennings spoke at the closing ceremony of the 2006 American Crossword Puzzle Tournament, the same year a near-finished cut of *Wordplay* was given a special screening. There seemed to be widespread agreement among those who saw the film that Ken Burns had gone over the top with his claim that we solve crosswords because we live our lives in boxes, from apartment blocks to the gridwork of city streets. The audience roared with derisive laughter as he pushed the metaphor to the brink.

"I don't want to get all Ken Burns–y and pretentious," Jennings began, waiting a beat for the applause to die down before he continued, "but there is a strain of slight anti-intellectualism in the country today. It gets a lot of reality shows green-lighted, and it gets presidents elected from time to time. But I think it's nice sometimes to have a reminder that knowledge is important. Knowing words, knowing names, knowing facts. It's valuable—helps you out in innumerable ways. It's always better to know a thing than not to know it. I'm always grateful for *Jeopardy!* and crosswords that remind America of that. Yeah, pat yourselves on the back. You're the keepers of the flame."

Remember That "Holy Tango" Is an Anagram of "Anthology"

I chose to observe Francis in the act of making a puzzle for a few different reasons. He is funny and smart, and his extracurricular talents extend far beyond crosswords. There's his book *Holy Tango of Literature*, the premise of which is to rearrange the letters of a famous writer's name and then use the anagram as the title for a parody of that writer's work. The concept is genius and he pulls it off with great skill. He has written a musical, both lyrics and music. He tap dances.

Francis works a day job as an editor of crossword puzzles for Sterling Publishing, and the persnicketiness it requires in no way thwarts his boundary-pushing creativity. On the contrary, it fuels him. Someone who thrives on these constraints is well positioned to make accomplished puzzles, and Francis has published several titles of his own crosswords (and, to my dismay, sudoku puzzles, although, true to form, he managed to devise witty pop culture tie-ins, from *Snakes on a Sudoku* to *The Sudoku Code*).

His puzzles appear every eight weeks in the *Onion*, a venue he hoped would allow him to experiment with creating a new, free-wheeling language for writing clues. Limited space has prevented him from pulling out the stops.

Francis has made all kinds of crosswords: the typical daily 15 x 15 grid; the Sunday-size 21 x 21; themed and themeless; symmetrical and asymmetrical; naughty and G-rated. As he sat down at his PC, the first question was: What kind of crossword will we make today?

Quod Me Nutrit Me Destruit

These are the words Angelina Jolie has tattooed below her navel. Translated from Latin, they mean: "That which nourishes me destroys me." Is this her way of signaling to the world that she, too, is addicted to crosswords?

This phrase turns out to be a favorite slogan of the eating-disorder community. I say we're kindred spirits. Be it food or crosswords, we're discussing the same thing: an aspect of life that we can control. When chaos looms all around, some refuse to eat, and we turn to the puzzle. Not only does it shut out the craziness, but we are focused on a task we know we can master. It's not about whether we'll complete it, it's about how much solace we can get out of immersing ourselves in it. If there were a chance we could not finish the crossword, we wouldn't do it.

This is what I used to say—until the time came when I had to cheat to fill in a tough corner. In so doing, I became, for that day, one of those people for whom the puzzle is itself the source of anxiety, not its vanquisher. Knowing that others struggled with the same clues provided little comfort. Actually, no comfort at all. That's their business. I still hated myself.

Birth of a Notion

In 1913, America cultivated the seedlings of its two major contributions to twentieth-century global culture: the Hollywood feature was born when Samuel Goldwyn and Cecil B. DeMille shot *The Squaw Man*, released through what would become the first major studio; and the next incarnation of the popular music theretofore known as ragtime was given a new name, "jazz," by a San Francisco newspaper.

In that same year, 1913, the world was coming apart at the seams. Pablo Picasso depicted a guitar by breaking down and rearranging its component parts. Igor Stravinsky, borrowing a technique used by film editors, did away with thematic development and strung together a montage of discrete snippets to make *The Rite of Spring*. Niels Bohr proposed that the universe itself is made up of unimaginably tiny bits. Time and space were not quite what we thought they were.

As the year drew to a close, Arthur Wynne, a Liverpool-born journalist working in New York, stripped words from their sentences, and thus their contexts, reducing them to their smallest units of meaning, and then he organized them into an appealing collection of interlocking facts, creating a new pastime from which satisfaction was derived by taking the verbal splinters of life and putting them back together again. In so doing he created a new American gift to the world that would eventually reach as many people as movies and jazz, exportable to any place on the globe with a language whose words are composed of individual letters.

Headlines in the December 21, 1913, Edition of the New York *World*

DUNN IS CONVICTED BY JURY IN FIRST ROAD GRAFT TRIAL

Tammany Contractor, His Company and Foreman Fogarty of Highways Department Found Guilty of Conspiracy to Defraud State in Building Section of Tuxedo Turnpike

PHONE STOCK RISES, MARKET BOOMS, ON COMPROMISE NEWS

A.T.&T. Shares Jump 7 Points in First Few Minutes of Frenzied Trading on Exchange — Brokers Swamped with Buying Orders — Old Fashioned Bull Movement Expected.

BOY FALLS 7 STORIES OFF ROOF AND LIVES

He Gets Only Slight Concussion of Brain and Bruised Arm In 80-Foot Plunge

GUN AT HER HEAD, WOMAN ROBBED IN YONKERS STREET

Highwayman Halters Her in Front of Frank Hedley's Home and Steals Bag Containing Farm Deed and Jewels.

On the Origin of a Species

Shaped like a diamond, the "word-cross" made its debut without fanfare on Sunday, December 21, 1913, in the New York *World*'s Fun supplement, a weekly compendium of brain teasers, cartoons, and "jokes." It occupied a space that had featured a word search one week, a maze the next, an anagram puzzle the week after that.

By today's standards, the word-cross of December 21 is a disgrace. Four squares hang out to dry at each point with no words to cross them. There's an instance of disagreement between verb tenses: "To sink in mud" is the clue for MIRED, prompting British crossword maker and historian Don Manley to call it "a duff clue," in the very first puzzle no less. The answer DOVE appears not once but twice, clued first as "A bird" and then later as "A pigeon." And several obscurities show up, including "The fibre of the gomuti palm," whose answer, DOH, would not gain cultural currency until the birth, seventy-six years later, of Homer Simpson.

These complaints are possible only in retrospect, thanks to a set of rules and expectations that took hold over the subsequent decades. For some reason, though, Wynne's invention somehow distinguished itself to its audience, and so it made an encore appearance.

"The great interest shown in FUN's word-cross puzzle, published last week, has prompted the puzzle editor to submit another of the same kind."

What constitutes "great interest"? History does not relate. Known in the business as a fudge phrase, "great interest" could mean anything from a deluge of letters to a favorable comment by a copyboy on Monday morning. But something more powerful than public relations had to have been at work here, because this new creation then appeared for a third week.

"Find the Missing Cross Words" read the headline on January 4, 1914. The transposition is generally attributed to printer's error, perhaps because the copy below it invited readers to solve "another of FUN's word-cross puzzles." It may well have been a mistake, but to my mind it could just as easily have resulted from the natural fluidity that occurs when a creative concept is in its infancy, when stakes are low.

Regardless of the cause, by January 11, the new name had stuck. The headline proclaimed "FUN's Cross-Word Puzzle," the text below conformed, and the cross-word continued to appear on a weekly basis.

"FUN's cross-word puzzles apparently are getting more popular than ever. The puzzle editor has received from readers many interesting new cross-word puzzles, which he will be glad to use from time to time. It is more difficult to make up a cross-word puzzle than it is to solve one. If you doubt this try to make one yourself."

The editor obliged the following week by printing a puzzle contributed by Mrs. M. B. Wood of New York City. The crossword had taken hold. But why? What was it about Wynne's invention that set it apart from its precursors? The crossword combines elements of word forms that were popular in the nineteenth century—the word square, the double acrostic—and yet it is much more than just an incremental development. Something about the crossword represented a leap in evolution, the birth of a new species, one that would outlast all others and not only survive but thrive into a new millennium.

Advertisements in the New York *World* During the Winter of 1913–14

LET ME REMOVE YOUR
GOITRE
$2.50 TEST TREATMENT
FREE

———

Are You
FAT?
I Was ONCE.
I Reduced
MYSELF.

———

INVESTING FOR PROFIT
FREE

———

FREE
HEAD NOISES
TREATMENT

———

SONG
POEMS WANTED

———

FITS
$2.50 TREATMENT FREE
Men, women and children
all over this country
have been permanently
relieved of fits,
epilepsy and fainting
spells by the wonderful
restorative treatment
perfected by the
venerable Dr. P_____
of Battle Creek, Mich.

PILES
This remarkable internal
remedy will prove to
you that an operation is
unnecessary.

FREE TO ASTHMA
SUFFERERS
A New Home Cure That
Anyone Can Use Without
Discomfort or Loss of Time

Rheumatism
A Home Cure Given by One
Who Had It

OPIUM or Morphine Habit
Treated. Free trial.

This Happy Wife
Wishes to Tell You Free
HOW SHE STOPPED
Her Husband's Drinking

Your Bunion Can Be Cured
Instant Relief
Prove It At My Expense

Cured His RUPTURE

HOW TO MAKE LOVE
(NEW BOOK) Tells How To
Get Acquainted; How to
Begin Courtship; How to
Court a Bashful Girl; to
Woo a Widow; to win an
Heiress; how to catch a
Rich Bachelor; how to
manage your beau to make
him propose; how to make
your fellow or girl love
you; what to do before
and after the wedding.
Tells other things

necessary for Lovers to
know. Sample copy by mail
10 cents.

RADIZENE WILL HELP YOU
GET NEW HAIR

QUIT Tobacco

CATARRH
FREE ADVICE ON ITS CURE
• • •
LEARN AT ONCE HOW TO
CURE CATARRH

GREY-HAIRED AT 27
NOT A GREY HAIR AT 35

FAT is Danger

Since John
Quit Drinking
By John's Wife

FRECKLES
Now Is the Time to Get Rid
of These Ugly Spots.

BEAUTIFUL BUST
How to Get a PERFECT FORM
50¢ Box
FREE

Christmastime 2007, Nearly Three Years After Sudoku Took the Country by Storm and Everyone Wondered if It Was Just a Flash in the Pan or Here to Stay, These Are the Featured Titles at the Bookloft in Great Barrington, Massachusetts

Will Shortz, *Sudoku for 365 Days*
The Original Sudoku
More Original Sudoku
Sudoku for Dummies
Will Shortz, *The Little Red and Green Book of Crosswords*

Submitted with Humility (And a Fair Amount of Trepidation)

Anyone who has witnessed the opening of the American Crossword Puzzle Tournament knows that one points out errors in the *Times* crossword at one's peril. The 2005 tournament began on the very day the puzzle included a marvel of misdirection: 1-Down, "They got back on the road in 1998." If you had solved all but the third crossing down clue, you would be looking at B E _ T L E S . Before the end of the day, Will Shortz had already received a note from a reader expressing disdain. Everyone knew the Beatles had disbanded nearly three decades earlier. (I was reminded of Paul McCartney's line that there would be no reunion as long as John Lennon remained dead.) Shortz was pitch-perfect as he captured the moral outrage of the letter—and then gently deflated it as he pointed out that the actual answer, BEETLES, as in Volkswagen, was correct all along.

I've learned to assume over the years that if I spot something that looks wrong, it's a good idea to look a second, third, and even a fourth time. Usually, I'm the one who's just not seeing things the right way.

Then, on the morning of September 23, 2005, when I encountered 52-Down, "'As It Happens' airer," I didn't think twice before entering CBC (all the while wondering if the Canadian Broadcasting Corporation had in fact been broadcasting its long-running interview program during the lockout that crippled the network during that time). This, however, resulted in a suspicious C-N combination in the crossing entry.

Aha! I thought, Will Shortz and the constructor, Levi

Denham, must be thinking of the entity that broadcasts the show south of the border. And indeed they were. They got the wrong one, though. While NPR (the answer in that day's puzzle) does air interesting news programs, it is American Public Media, a division of Minnesota Public Radio, that distributes *As It Happens* in the United States. Because NPR is the oldest and the most famous of the three major syndicators of public radio programming in the United States (the other two being PRI and the aforementioned APM), it has become the Kleenex of its industry. And it's natural to want National Public Radio and "national public radio" to be synonymous. They are not.

Shortz's e-mailed response: "Yup, you got me on 'As It Happens.'—Will."

You might think that spotting an error in the *New York Times* crossword would give a thrill. Surprisingly, it didn't.

On Solving the Crossword Without a Stopwatch

That settles it. Racing against the clock ruins the experience.

On a Monday, I timed myself while solving the *Times* crossword, thinking it would be good training for the annual American Crossword Puzzle Tournament. I didn't even notice the theme, which was organized around the concept of twos.

The next day I decided to do the puzzle just for fun. And that's exactly what it was. Time slipped away. I entered my happy place. I developed a deep appreciation for the constructor, Nancy Salomon. The elegance of her mind set off fireworks in mine. The grid somehow seemed to engulf me, and I became attentive to the full pleasure of the experience in all its anatomy.

I hear the cries of sour grapes: because I don't stand a chance of ever winning the tournament, I've concocted an elaborate justification for why I should not try.

Maybe. But the lyric that burrowed its way into my head is: "I want a man with a slow hand."

The Terror of a Blank Canvas

Francis told me he *only* solves crosswords against the clock, and that doing so does not diminish his enjoyment of the clues. I find this almost impossible to believe, but then I am forced to consider that his brain whirs at many more rpm than mine. Francis consistently ranks near the top at the American Crossword Puzzle Tournament. In 2007 and 2009 he came in third.

Francis fired up his Dell, a beater. Like many things in Francis's world, it boasts vintage cred. It is charming, for sure, but exudes questionable trustworthiness.

As many constructors do, Francis uses a software program called Crossword Compiler. These days, anyone who sits down at a table with pencil and paper to make a puzzle is mugging for the camera. Because of computers, it is much easier to construct what is known as a wide open grid. Rarely does anyone have to rely on extra black squares—known in the biz as cheaters—to fit the pieces together. Computers can easily figure out how to stack three fifteen-letter answers on top of one another, something that appears more and more these days. What aficionados find pleasing in this regard is no doubt lost on the large majority of average solvers.

There is no shame in letting computers do the drudge work of fitting words together. They are much better and faster at it than humans are. Francis could contemplate endless grid formations with his mouse. This is both a good thing and a bad thing. I have experienced this freedom using audio-editing software for my radio work. Time evaporates as you try out one cross-fade after another. Radio deadlines being what they are, the curse outweighs the blessing here. Francis reports it is quite easy to lose track of time while making a grid. This would become evident soon enough, and Francis no doubt had as much in mind when he proposed the plan of action.

"Why don't I have some lunch, first?" Francis said. "Walk with me to the corner and get a sandwich?"

Rehab, Hospital for Special Surgery

I look over and am fairly certain the man sitting next to me in the waiting room is the art critic Robert Hughes. He is struggling with the *Times* crossword. I try to make small talk, offering that I struggled with the trick employed for that particular puzzle. He swats me away with a mumble about how he struggles with the puzzle every morning. I don't know if he is usually this grumpy or if it has to do with the reason I presume he is here: seven years earlier, Hughes was in a car crash that nearly killed him. Since I have suffered only a fracture to the fibula as the result of a midnight bicycle ride in the mud, I can't really hold it against him. His remark reminds me, however, that Norman Mailer once claimed to have trouble solving the *Times* crossword on Saturdays. A year after my encounter in the hospital, Mailer dies. His obituaries all coalesce around his tendency toward braggadocio and ignore this acknowledgment of his own humility.

The Man at the End of the Road

The man at the end of the road stares at me every time I go by. He has rugged features, and his penetrating eyes seem to indicate a deep intelligence. At first glance he looks a little like Samuel Beckett, but a closer look reveals that no, his is the empty, scowling, uncomprehending gaze of Don Imus.

He sits in a folding lawn chair, his winter coat buttoned up to his neck and a wool cap pulled over his ears. Even on warm days. Sometimes he walks in circles in his front yard, other times he waves and gives a nod. Once, as I rode by on my bicycle, he applauded as if I were Lance Armstrong.

A few times he has wandered toward my house. There's almost no problem with burglary in the Berkshires, and many people don't lock their doors, but I've started to do it out of fear he'll show up while I'm out and get hold of a carving knife I've left on the counter. When I had to replace my septic system, he became so curious about the large equipment that landed in my backyard, it was too easy to imagine him hopping on the backhoe and undoing three days' work, and maybe himself.

My second-worst fear in the world is that I will end up like him. (The worst is just the opposite—that my mind will remain intact but trapped inside a body that is unable to move or talk. Should that time ever come, I hope someone will hook me up to a computer that can translate brain waves into language so that I will be able to say, "Pull the plug now please right away thank you good-bye.")

When it comes to the battle against senility, the media would have you believe that, as the sweepstakes envelope says, you may already be a winner, and that you have crossword puzzles to thank. The humble crossword is now a crucial weapon in the baby boomer's arsenal against aging.

The *Times* of London: "Use It or Lose It: How Crosswords Can Beat Alzheimer's."

Katie Couric quizzing Dr. Yaakov Stern, director of Columbia University's Cognitive Neuroscience Division, on "some exciting new developments that could offer real help to people at risk of developing Alzheimer's disease . . . If you participate in leisure activities that are sort of—stimulate your brain, that is obviously helpful. But that—that seems like that's not necessarily a new finding. Is it, Dr. Stern?"

"Well, that's something we've known for a while, that people with higher education, more stimulating jobs . . ."

"Crossword puzzles," Couric says.

"Crossword puzzles."

An *Esquire* reader asks Dr. Oz for Free Advice from a Medical Professional: "Why can't I remember a damned thing?" The doctor responds that the brain needs exercise. "Stimulate it by traveling outside your normal environment and by doing things like crossword puzzles."

Half of his answer is suspect, and the other half is dead-on, in ways the doctor himself has perhaps not considered.

It is now an article of faith that crosswords will help you hold on to whatever brains Mozart gave you when you were an infant. As memes go, this one is appealing. David (the crossword) slays Goliath (dementia), and we can all stop worrying. See? Alzheimer's isn't so scary after all.

It is too good to be true.

Nevertheless, publishers see an opportunity and seize it. The American Association of Retired Persons starts issuing a series of puzzle books:

> *Awesome Crosswords to Keep You Sharp*
> *Baffling Crosswords to Keep You Sharp*

The *New York Times* creates its own series:

> *Crosswords for a Brain Workout*
> *Crosswords to Exercise Your Brain*
> *Crosswords to Boost Your Brainpower*

Puzzle editor Will Shortz, in his introduction to *Fitness for the Mind Crosswords, Vol. 1: 100 Crossword Puzzles to Keep Your Brain in Shape*, makes powerful claims on behalf of the pastime he's done so much to promote in America. "Far from being a waste of time," he writes, "it's been shown to have many practical benefits, especially among older people." He cites two reports in particular that conclude crosswords can reduce the risk of Alzheimer's. One is from *Senior Health News*. The other, from the *Journal of the American Medical Association*, concerns the famous nun study in Minnesota, in which almost seven hundred School Sisters of Notre Dame in Mankato shared their writing, their life stories, and even their postmortem brains with researchers looking into the subtle ways in which verbal expression and physical health relate to dementia.

Shortz goes on, "Of course, all mental exercise is good. Crosswords, however, are especially good for you, because they give the brain an all-round workout. They test your vocabulary, knowledge, mental flexibility and sometimes even your sense of humor. They're the mental equivalent of going to a gym and working out on all the machines, not just the StairMaster or weights."

I wonder.

To visit Dr. Joe Verghese is to empathize with the rat in the Skinner box. A maze of halls leads to his office at Albert Einstein College of Medicine in the Bronx, where he studies the relationship between aging and mental decline. Many news reports concerning crosswords and senility arose from the study he led. While the headlines he inspired are declarative and blunt, he is nuanced and quiet. I have to tilt my head closer to hear him.

His team's conclusion: based on their study of 469 people over the age of 75, "participation in leisure activities is associated with a reduced risk of dementia." In their report, published in June of 2003, he and his colleagues singled out four activities—reading, playing board games, playing musical instruments, and dancing.

Not crosswords.

Those, he told me, "were actually borderline in their usefulness." Still, reporters grabbed onto the idea that crosswords keep dementia at bay—perhaps because the editors of the *New England Journal of Medicine* chose to print a graph that mentioned them, or maybe just because they make for a provocative headline.

Ultimately, it matters little where crosswords and dancing appear on a scale of usefulness. The bigger issue is a pervasive fuzzy thinking when it comes to cause-and-effect relationships. To say that leisure activities are *associated* with a reduced risk of dementia is not the same as saying they are *responsible* for it. This rather major distinction is often lost in the quick and dirty world of headline writing, ever-shrinking news cycles, and certainly in the game of telephone that happens any time someone recounts the news heard with one ear while on the way to drinks with friends.

Even if crosswords are only marginally associated with a reduced risk of dementia, Dr. Verghese was willing to offer three possibilities for why that might be the case.

The first has nothing at all to do with causality. Instead, it's possible that crosswords are simply a marker of a generally healthy lifestyle. Perhaps people who are naturally inclined to eat well and exercise are also likely to do puzzles.

The second does deal in causality, but once removed. Crosswords may be beneficial because they reduce stress. Stress produces cortisol, and cortisol shrinks the hippocampus. Of course, for people who are terrified by crosswords, solving them *creates* stress, which may account for the marginal association between puzzles and dementia.

For the third possibility, Dr. Verghese outlined the theory of cognitive reserve, which he described as a "mental buffer against disease that conceals the effects of dementia." According to this scenario, by attaining many more marbles earlier in life, when you do start to lose them, it takes longer to notice it.

My lifelong interest in crosswords has nothing to do with adult worries about losing my marbles. I began solving as a teenager, a time when no one considers the possibility of life without marbles. This once-innocent pastime has now been saddled with a new utilitarian purpose, and each encounter with the puzzle is freighted with meaning. At best it's an inoculation against Alzheimer's; at worst, a graphic daily reminder of the inevitable downward slide. There are days when squares must be left blank. Evidence of amyloid plaques forming in the brain, no?

I've started to count the times people have had to finish my sentences for me and notice myself covering for it by adopting a strategy I've learned from stutterers, who look ahead at what they're about to utter and change direction to avoid words they know will cause them trouble.

When I discuss these worries with friends, they find me ridiculous to the point of embarrassment. Everyone forgets things, they say. They're not up on the latest thinking that says, no, mental decline is not an inevitable part of the aging process. Several friends cite the fact that I am able to complete the *Times* crossword at all. To people like them, this means I have plenty of marbles, and wanting any more is greedy. I try to explain that what matters is not how I compare to others but how I stack up relative to my own past performance. This gets me nowhere, and they write me off as a hypochondriac.

The outcome I wish for is that they are right and it's all in my head. I develop my own corollary to Pascal's Wager:

I'm skeptical about whether solving crossword puzzles fights dementia, but I figure it couldn't hurt. And so I finish at least one puzzle, sometimes two, every day. This once-pleasurable diversion becomes joyless, dutiful.

Until it becomes difficult.

Black Friday: July 28, 2006. The second hardest puzzle of the week, constructed on this day by Sherry O. Blackard.

I start working on it the night before, shortly after 10 PM eastern time, when the *Times* makes its puzzles available online. I have little trouble filling in the upper left-hand corner.

And then, nothing. I am simply unable to fill in anything else. Maybe it's because I'm tired, so I make strategic use of a phenomenon mentioned by MSNBC's Keith Olbermann: "Psychologists refer to it informally as the 'crossword puzzle effect.' You're trying to fill out a crossword puzzle but you're stumped [by] a couple of clues and you give up and move on to do something else. Minutes, hours, even days later, the answer will suddenly come to you. The point is your mind has kept working on the problem even if consciously you have not been." Research I conduct yields no evidence that psychologists refer to the crossword puzzle effect, but Olbermann does describe something real, so I put the puzzle aside, feeling confident I'll get through it the next morning once I've had a good night's sleep.

The next morning. No luck. I sit there, stuck, in a coffee bar that I frequent because of the lattes and despite the music. On this day, the stereo offers up one cut after another from a compilation I've named "Songs I Spent the Seventies and Eighties Trying to Shut Out of My Mind."

Panic, soundtrack provided by Chicago: "If you leave

me now, you'll take away the biggest part of me." I notice my heart starting to race. If I didn't know better I'd swear I could feel my body producing cortisol, that brain-shrinking stress hormone, which, you may remember, is exactly what we don't want to happen. For some reason, I have always attached special importance to knowing things, and gaps in my knowledge tend to bring on an especially potent feeling of inadequacy. Perhaps a psychologist would say it's the result of being deprived of love as a child, but whatever the cause, I try my best to hide this defect from others. This morning it's riding me hard. Under normal circumstances, to avoid a tailspin like this one, the puzzle must be put aside. I decide instead to push back like a marathoner running through the pain.

Ultimately it is a simple act of will that ends this sorry episode. Maybe it's the torture of Toni Tennille singing "Muskrat Love." I won't allow myself to get up from the table until the puzzle is finished. I sit there, reminding myself of the feeling I usually have: I can do this. And, as it turns out, I can, but not without being sorely shaken in the process.

As usual, being stuck results from looking at a clue the wrong way. Once I fix that, the rest of the puzzle falls like a decrepit barn in a heavy wind. Maybe I owe a debt of gratitude to some primal instinct kicking in to protect me from having to hear one more of these songs. Finally, I fill in the last square just as Bob Seger asks, "Why don't you stay?" Thank you, no.

My growing concerns about marble loss prompt me to send $75 to San Clemente, California. (The habitual crossworder in me automatically lists the associations that come to mind: Nixon; young press aide Diane Sawyer running with scissors and colliding with the ex-president; Dan Aykroyd calling John Belushi "Jew boy"; clemency.)

Days later I receive a package from the Memory Fitness Institute containing Dr. Gary Small's *Memory Bible* DVD (as seen on PBS!), his "best-selling book" *The Memory Bible*, another called *The Memory Prescription*, and a board game called Senior Moments.

The DVD's homespun label does not inspire confidence. The program is an infomercial featuring Dr. Small attempting humor—senility jokes were never funny in the first place—in front of a live studio audience. Before long the disk starts to sputter, refusing to track properly in my DVD player. One minute, there is a shot of Dr. Small and a crossword puzzle, and then nothing. I consider trying another machine but rule out this option because of the doctor's fondness for bad puns.

An online questionnaire determines what subjective impressions I have of my own memory. All in all, I think I'm doing okay. Then comes the objective memory test. In two minutes I must remember ten words: violin, balloon, stereo, building, strawberry, cradle, mast, lizard, teacher, oven. I set my kitchen timer, hit the start button, and repeat the words over and over. Having spent my life in radio and music, it's safe to say that I learn best through my ears. As the seconds tick away, I start chanting rhythmically, breaking them into groups of three and four. Violinballoonstereo. Buildingstrawberrycradle. Mastlizardteacheroven.

Time's up.

I'm then directed to spend the next twenty minutes thinking of something else. I make several phone calls—

to update my insurance policy, change a doctor's appointment—and when that's done I do a little light reading about synaptic plasticity. I do whatever I can to pass the time without thinking about those ten words—until the timer rings and I must write down as many of them as I can recall.

Violin, balloon, stereo.

Strawberry.

Closet.

Mask?

Closet, mask.

That's all I've got. I look at the list. MAST! Not mask. And where the hell did I get closet? From cradle? *God damn it.*

Up pops a screen called Your Memory Assessment Summary. "You were able to learn and recall 4 words, which indicates that you are experiencing some challenges in your everyday memory tasks before initiating any of *The Memory Bible* techniques."

Thanks for reminding me.

"Your scores indicate that you are experiencing some memory challenges."

Yes, I figured that part out.

Small's *Memory Bible* offers various techniques for improving your memory. Is this memory, though, or just workarounds?

Small argues they're the same thing, and indeed that was how it seemed when Tatiana Cooley-Marquardt, a repeat winner of the USA National Memory Championship, demonstrated her tricks to me. To memorize ten playing cards, she assigns a word to each card. These aren't just random words; she picks them according to the cards' value and suit. Those words form a sentence that is borderline nonsensical but has more meaning than a string of random data. By creating a personal connection to the cards, she can "remember" them.

It still doesn't feel like memory, though. It seems more like the fallback position, the glass we break in case of emergency when memory fails. I wonder if Small is right. Are these tricks in fact how memory itself works? When struggling to find an obscure crossword answer, I enter a free-associative state. If the pathway I'm following is blocked, maybe I'll have access to another. Let's say a puzzle requires the name of a movie actress who was immortalized in song by a pop band in the 1980s, and I just cannot for the life of me remember her name. I remember she has a sister, but her name also escapes me at the moment and is therefore of no use. And then I remember that her father—or was it her grandfather?—was in show business, too. Wasn't he on *Hollywood Squares*? Yes, that's right. And then I visualize the tic-tac-toe board and see Paul Lynde in the middle square. And then my mind's eye scans down to the lower left-hand corner and I see Charley Weaver and remember that was the stage name of—someone named Arquette. I don't remember his first name, but I don't need to, because once I have the family name it comes to me: ROSANNA.

Fresh Fill Wanted

Francis decided on a grid, but because he was using a computer, that grid remained in a constantly fluid state until the last fill was entered.

This term always brings landfill to mind, and it does indeed betray the hierarchy of crossword answers. You have your theme entries, which come first, and then the fill, which accommodates them. There are themeless puzzles, but still they tend to be organized around larger, symmetrically placed answers that function similarly to theme entries.

Describing fill in this way makes it seem unimportant, but just the opposite is true: it is the fill that separates the good puzzles from the bad. Ask Will Shortz what he looks for in submissions and his first answer is always "fresh fill." This is how he helped bring about the revolution in crosswords when he took over as the *Times* puzzle editor: by eliminating, as much as possible, crosswordese—that absurdly specific vocabulary of obscure words and names that were the mainstay of his predecessors' puzzles—and replacing it with fresh fill, the ancillary words that pop out at you instead of overstaying their welcome like a Celebes ox (ANOA).

Even though Francis's computer inspires as much confidence as the *Millennium Falcon*, he was able to instantly try out any possibility he wanted. He'd put in a word, click his mouse, and immediately see a set of possible crossings. Click it again, and another set appeared.

The downside of modernity: you can spot computer-generated fill, which is why the top constructors spend time maintaining their databases. That means taking out the default crosswordese, putting in words or phrases of your own—Francis thinks he just might be the only constructor with DONDIXON, the musician who produced REM, in his database—and then ranking them all according to desirability, with low numbers going to fill you'd use only as a last resort.

Self-respecting constructors write their own clues.

Footnote to History

Olsher's Law: Wacky news gets the headline; the refutation gets buried. This was true when the Mozart effect was shown to be a fallacy, and it was true when brain researchers published a study, unsexily titled "Predictors of Crossword Puzzle Proficiency and Moderators of Age-Cognition Relations." Issued by David Hambrick, Timothy Salthouse, and Elizabeth Meinz in 1999, it is really a metastudy—research looking into the research of others. They came to two interesting conclusions. The first:

> [G]eneral knowledge is the strongest predictor of crossword puzzle proficiency. Surprisingly, abstract reasoning ability, as measured by several different tests, had no direct relation to puzzle proficiency.

But it's their second conclusion that really should, though it never will, grab the attention of editors and headline writers:

> The results provide no evidence to suggest that amount of crossword puzzle experience reduces age-related decreases in fluid cognition or enhances age-related increases in crystallized cognition.

Put simply, crossword puzzles will not prevent you from losing your mind.

Bad Things Happen When You Leave the City

It becomes more and more difficult to think of fresh and creative birthday presents for my father. Our running joke revolves around not knowing what to get the man who has everything. As he approached his seventieth birthday and I was immersed in research about crosswords, I made him a gift of several books by my favorite constructors, including a *Sit and Solve* book by Francis featuring a toilet seat on the cover.

I was already suspicious of the claim that crosswords prevent Alzheimer's, but maybe I was subconsciously fashioning Pascal to suit the occasion. What was the harm, after all?

You could say the harm is in potentially raising false hopes. How long before angry, senile people start demanding their money back from Will Shortz?

The fact is, I was worried about my father's memory. Our e-mail threads are littered with his complaints that I leave him in the dark about what I'm up to, followed by me pointing to the electronic paper trail. Him, insisting I never mentioned anything about a residency at an artists' colony and that he had to look it up to find out what it was. Me, cutting and pasting, showing how I had mentioned it first here, and then again here and once again here.

I was glad, while visiting him in Florida, to see several of the crossword books lying about in various states of being solved. Seeing them prompted me to bring up something that happened the year before.

He asked me what I was talking about.

You remember, when I visited last year while you were in the middle of moving. Remember the boxes all around?

He didn't. He had no recollection at all that I had been there. This was a whole different category of memory loss. Forgetting what you read in an e-mail, even in three different e-mails, can be explained. Perhaps it never really registered because, unlike the trained memory champs, my father wasn't able to make an emotional connection to it. But this was not abstract information that I had recounted from my life in an e-mail. It was something that had happened to him. And no amount of pleading could make the difference.

Now, when I imagine my father working on a crossword, Pascal's Wager is the furthest thing from my mind. I'm just glad the puzzles provide him with a pleasant way to pass the time.

One of the stories my father liked to repeat throughout my childhood had to do with people who, as World War II seemed more likely, conducted thorough research and determined that the safest place to wait things out was the island of Guam. They moved there just in time to find out they couldn't have been more wrong.

This story always had the ring of urban myth, even when I was little. Which "people," exactly? Still, the lesson seemed sound: You think you're so smart, trying to escape fate. Good luck with that one.

My dad has always loved morality tales. But this one he ignored. When he lived on Florida's Atlantic coast and two hurricanes had destroyed his neighbors' property but not his, he moved inland. It made sense that he would settle in The Villages—a manufactured reality of theme-park town squares, manicured lawns, and identical houses. This community is all about safety, down to the gates that keep out the under-55 riffraff. Lately Dad's been sending e-mails about how he's finally getting the retirement he's always wanted: "I love it here. Everything is taken care of for you."

It seemed like the perfect place to live out the remainder of a life that was in many ways determined by fear: from the early days, when unpredictable change and rising crime prompted his parents to flee the Bronx, through his own parenting years devoted to teaching me lessons about household safety, including the frequent reminder that electricity and water make for a lethal combination.

We spent several days driving through The Villages, sometimes in his car, other times in his golf cart. There were long silences. He filled them with a tour guide's list of the different house models, starting with more modest styles like his and going all the way up to the million-dollar homes that lined the golf courses.

"They really went first-class all the way."

Then, more silence. He pointed to the sites where all the new buildings would be going up: a motel, doctors' offices, Walmart. I tried to smile and feign interest, but he made it clear I had failed.

"I realize this probably doesn't interest you. I just don't know what you like." What I didn't say out loud is that I would have liked to see the trees and the farms that used to be there.

"Look at all this. Just five years ago, this was nothing," he snarled, as if that nothingness deserved contempt.

The night before I flew home I couldn't sleep. I lay in bed and thought about the 67,000 people (and counting) who had come to this place to escape real life. No doubt it suited them as much as it did my father. It felt to me as if I had already died.

Within hours, though, I was feeling more alive than

ever. This happens whenever you come too close to having life suddenly snatched away.

First came the sudden warm air, which prompted me to turn on the ceiling fan for the first time after a week of unseasonably cold temperatures. Then came the electric storm—rapid flashes of bright white light in the window, with no pause between lightning strike and thunderclap.

And then came the sound of a jet engine speeding toward the house.

The word *tornado* did not enter my head when, at three o'clock in the morning, that jet-engine sound engulfed my father's house and touched the button in my lizard brain marked DANGER! RUN FOR YOUR LIFE! which instinctively moved me away from the window and toward an interior doorway.

Why a doorway? That's what Dad always told me when I was a kid. Folk wisdom has gotten smarter since then. Now people bring pillows and blankets into their "safe rooms." I've filed this away for next time.

I saw a flash of amber light. Was it a transformer exploding on the power line behind the house, probably blasting PCBs into the air? Or was it the bulb flaming out as plywood from someone's roof shattered the window next to mine and knocked the lamp to the floor?

Inexplicably, my father walked toward the window, while the jet-engine winds were still roaring, to inspect the damage and put up what he called "hurricane shutters"— unconvincing panels of plastic and Velcro.

"Yes," I told him. "The windows are shattered. But the storm is still dangerous. You know, barn doors and horses and all."

At this point he decided it was a good idea to unplug the lamp—the very lamp that was still getting rained on.

"No, Dad, we're going to turn off the circuit break-ers before . . ." But I was too late. Had he forgotten all of those warnings he delivered during my childhood? Was he in shock? Was this the return of another favorite slogan of his—Do as I say, not as I do—that I'd spent my adult years trying to forget? Or were my fears about his men-tal condition more legitimate than I could have realized? I grabbed him by the arm and walked him into a utility closet to wait until the wind died down.

We were shaken, but a real feeling of dread hit us in the gut when the sun rose and Dad drove me to the airport. Two streets away, there were houses with large swaths of insulation where the siding should have been.

"Are these places still under construction?"

No, he said, dragging it out with a rising hint of worry mixed with gradual comprehension.

He drove around the corner, and we saw the trail left by the wind that had ripped roofs off homes and tore clear through newly built houses and left several neigh-bors dead. And then through the gates and past the con-struction site where, moments after dawn, workers were already stacking cinder blocks on the foundation for the new motel with renewed fierceness.

"It took so long to build this up, and it's gone in twenty minutes," he said. And then, another lesson: "Don't fool with Mother Nature."

Another lesson unlearned.

No doubt research will someday conclude with certainty that crosswords do or do not help to keep Alzheimer's at bay. But when it comes to understanding the relationship between puzzles and the mind, is this really the most interesting question to ask?

Neuroscience researchers tend to look into how the brain solves problems. I would like to know the answers to questions that science hasn't asked yet. Not "how?" but "why?" For example, what exactly is going on in the brain that draws such a huge number of us to solve crosswords in the first place? Will Shortz has various theories. One of them that he has shared with me more than once is that "people seem to like to fill in little boxes." This is an especially unsatisfying explanation. By this logic, we'd all race to finish our taxes the moment our W-2s arrive in January. Now that new technology such as functional Magnetic Resonance Imaging (fMRI) allows us to watch what happens in the brain over time, wouldn't it be instructive to know which parts light up while working on a puzzle?

Clinical researchers do not seem to share my priorities. For them, there are more urgent uses for the fMRI, like curing disease. This is understandable, but it is slightly sad, too, that we as a society tend to value things only for their practical purpose. When I reported on culture for NPR, it was heartbreaking to watch year after year as advocates made the well-meaning but ultimately cynical case that government should pay for the arts for pragmatic reasons like giving kids a competitive advantage in school or improving local economies. It's been unfashionable for a long time to talk about art for art's sake, and yet the optimist in me still hopes for the day when someone stands before Congress and asks it to support the NEA simply because having art in our lives makes us better human beings. When people resort to such desperate measures to save the arts, then the Republicans will already have won.

Something similar can be said about crosswords and senility. Soon after Alzheimer's and Parkinson's have been eliminated, I'd like to ask the neuroscientists of the world to turn their attention to puzzles, for the sake of pure knowledge. Use the fMRI and its progeny to find out what other activities light up the same parts of the brain as solving a puzzle. From the brain's point of view, is doing a crossword more or less the same as meditating? Or doing drugs? Or having sex?

It has become a tired trope for popular science writers over the last few years to put themselves in an fMRI, perform some mental task, and then describe the experience. Imagine my excitement when I read a book by Gregory Berns, a neuroscientist at Emory University School of Medicine in Atlanta. In *Satisfaction: The Science of Finding True Fulfillment*, Berns submits to an fMRI to demonstrate how the brain releases dopamine not only when we experience something rewarding (in his case, when he gets a taste of Kool-Aid through a feeder tube) but also when it *anticipates* a reward. A few chapters later he attends the American Crossword Puzzle Tournament and discusses the experience in terms of his research on dopamine.

The first baby steps toward an understanding of what processes in the brain drive us to solve puzzles.

For Berns, humans are drawn to crosswords not because they make us happy. The pleasure principle, he argues, is overrated. Instead, we are primarily motivated to create challenges for ourselves that we can overcome. This drive for satisfaction, which manifests itself whether we're solving puzzles, running marathons, or engaging in S&M (for some people, anyway), is hardwired into our brains.

Berns writes:

Satisfaction—that state of blessed contentment, nirvana, mystical enlightenment, peace, tranquility, a sense of something beyond your existence—is ephemeral at best. You get snatches of these states, often when you least expect them. Everything I have encountered inside the lab and out in the world suggests that satisfaction is not the same as either pleasure or happiness, and that searching for happiness will not necessarily lead to satisfaction. If anything, the feeling of being satisfied that I have sought comes from hard work, grappling with uncertainty, and sometimes pain. Nor is satisfaction the opposite of pleasure; it is something entirely different—a feeling unto itself.

This is the closest anyone has come to describing the experience of solving a crossword puzzle.

Until the time comes when science is advanced enough to help us interpret the blinking lights and the pretty pictures, we are left with natural-history observations, descriptions of experience.

"We are a generation from true understanding," said Ed Wolpow, a neuroscientist. Even though he is also a member of the National Puzzlers' League, he seemed dismissive of my interest, using words such as *trivia* and *arcana*.

It's hard to write something off as trivial if it takes up the time of more than 50 million Americans on a regular basis. Focusing instead on the positive, remember that *trivium* is the classical study of grammar, rhetoric, and logic, and *arcana* refers merely to secrets waiting to be revealed. Wolpow did nonetheless put me in touch with Alice Flaherty, a professor of neuroscience at Harvard Medical School, who shared what must still be considered speculation as to what drives a person to solve puzzles: "Three pathological models for the drive to do word puzzles are hypomania/mania, the temporal variant of frontotemporal dementia, and Asperger's syndrome."

The consensus is that the drive to solve word puzzles "almost certainly" results from their role in the release of dopamine, which can be addictive.

"The stuff we make in our brains can addict us," Wolpow said. "It doesn't have to be morphine or nicotine. I suppose that's behind some of our drives, like the sex drive, or hunger."

Berns writes at length about something that also came up in my conversation with Dr. Verghese, and that's novelty. We require it. Which is why Dr. Oz was on semisolid ground when he told the *Esquire* reader to stimulate his brain by "traveling outside your normal environment and by doing things like crossword puzzles." For a first-time solver, picking up a crossword is a novel experience, outside his or her normal environment. After years of doing them every day, it is anything but. True, there are always new things to be learned, but day after day, you're tilling the same row. I doubt you are creating any new synapses if you do the *New York Times* puzzle every day.

* * *

It's worth looking at the fallacies surrounding the aforementioned Mozart effect. Much ink was spent, along with millions of dollars, thanks to a study concluding that listening to a particular sonata by Mozart improved spatial reasoning skills in children, and that listening to music by Philip Glass did not. From the beginning it seemed preposterous (although not, apparently, to the governor of Georgia, who arranged in 1998 for every newborn in the state to receive a CD of Mozart's music). Music can make you joyous, pensive, bawl your eyes out, or dance around the room. But smarter? Come on.

Even the author of the original study has doubts. It may still be possible, though, that listening to Mozart is associated with improving test scores, for reasons that may someday shed light on the link between crosswords and senility. According to researchers in Toronto, the so-called Mozart effect has nothing to do with intelligence and everything to do with mood. The explanation may simply be that listening to Mozart makes many people happy, and an improved state of mind leads them to perform better on tests. This corresponds to Dr. Verghese's second theory that crosswords may help with dementia because they reduce stress. Fans of Philip Glass's music ought not despair: there is no reason to believe they are less intelligent than other music lovers. Maybe a little depressed, though.

I agree with Will Shortz that crosswords are far from a waste of time. It's just that the benefits are subtler than you might expect. I can't imagine that there is an immediately practical value to solving puzzles. Now, when I solve crosswords, I do it with the hope that I can retrieve that elusive state of mind, something I've experienced only a few times in my life.

It first happened while I was still in college, traveling alone through Europe during the summer, staring at Bruegel the Elder's *Land of Cockaigne* in Munich's Alte Pinakothek. The feeling was in no way brought on by the painting. It had nothing to do with what I was looking at but simply, and coincidentally, the accumulation of weeks spent alone, getting freshly acquainted with my own thoughts and mind in a way I had never done before.

It happened again roughly ten years later while I was leading a group of teenagers through six Eastern European countries in six weeks, stuck in a cramped and smelly microbus crossing Hungary's rolling hills for hours on end and with nothing left to say to one another.

Oh, and then there was the time about a dozen years after that, in the grocery-store parking lot when I was certain I was having the experience of living, as they say, in the moment. And then the moment was gone. I think it was somehow brought on by a billboard for the nursery next door, but I can't be sure.

In each instance, the static that normally occupies my headscape—snatches of conversation endlessly replayed, bits of recently heard music looped over and over—this noise was swept aside, and the receiver within my brain tuned in to a strong, clear signal. Suddenly, my thoughts spoke in a single, calm voice and in full sentences.

What was that? More important, how do I get it back?

I have experimented with meditation to quiet what the Buddhists call *monkey mind*. It hasn't taken. I'm simply too undisciplined. But in my dabbling, I have begun to suspect that people who meditate and people who solve crosswords are looking for the same thing. Whether focusing our attention on *om* or on 6-Down, we take control of that part of the brain that is normally hijacked by the voices telling us we're not good enough, smart enough, attractive enough. We silence those voices and channel their energy into a laserlike beam of thought aimed at empty spaces.

Is this true of any activity that absorbs us, like knitting or painting? It's possible. And if it turns out that crosswords serve a purpose simply because they are a kind of busywork, that's worth knowing. But I have to believe there is something about the harnessing of our language mechanism that makes crosswords such an effective anti-anxiety agent.

To describe crosswords as an escape or a distraction misses the point. I'd argue that the world, with its advertisements and petty jealousies and pursuit of money, is the distraction. Crosswords are the avenue back to that part within the self that needs regular care and attention. Crosswords are vital to our well-being.

When I pick up a puzzle I do my best to forget about memory loss and see it as a few minutes spent every day immersed in something bigger than the self, swimming in the ocean of the mind.

The crossword is a fiercely loyal friend. Lovers and employers will betray you, but the puzzle shows up every day. Unlike a dog, it has an indefinite life expectancy. The plane you're in that's about to take off cannot crash because in the universe within the grid, plane crashes don't exist. As long as your brain is consumed with dredging up ASTA, it can't be bothered to entertain ANGST.

River in Egypt

Francis continued to try out different grids—essentially an act of triage. Choosing one especially juicy entry for the northwest corner might force an infelicity in the middle. Words that begin or end with vowels, which are less common, should stay away from the edges, because that would force him to come up with yet more of these RARA AVIS words.

As Francis worked, he fielded instant messages from, among others, Peter Gordon, who is not only his boss at Sterling but also the editor of the crossword that used to appear in the now defunct *New York Sun*. Gordon was trying out a clue and wanted to know if Francis had ever heard of a band called the Urge. If anyone has heard of this band, it would be Francis, who performs and writes songs and possesses an encyclopedic knowledge of rock. He rendered a swift verdict.

"I feel if they were in existence while I was in college and I don't know them, yeah, that's a problem."

Francis went back to massaging the grid. His computer issued an ominous chord. Hitting the return key only made it sound again. The screen delivered the bad news: "Access Violation."

Francis was in denial. No matter how many times he touched the keyboard, the computer kept responding the same.

"This probably means I have to reboot."

Even after admitting the unhappy truth, Francis kept hitting the keys. The *Millennium Falcon* was equally stubborn.

"Stop it! I hate you!"

Finally we started writing down everything he had entered up to that point. Then Francis faced the inevitable and restarted the computer.

He sighed. "Crossword Compiler is not without its fatal bugs."

Crazy over Crosswords

In April of 1924, following the advice of columnist and crossword lover Franklin P. Adams, who worried that a book of puzzles would earn their new venture a frivolous reputation, Dick Simon and Max Schuster published their first title—*The Cross Word Puzzle Book*—under the Plaza imprint and watched it unexpectedly ignite a nationwide crossword craze. It was the birth of one of America's major publishing houses and also the longest continuous series of books in American history.

Songwriters of the time, always with a licked finger in the air to tell which way the wind was blowing, started putting out crossword-related numbers. Some engaged in simpleminded puns, such as "Cross Words Between Sweetie and Me" and "Cross Word Mamma You Puzzle Me (But Papa's Gonna Figure You Out)." From the beginning, crosswords seized the popular imagination as an object of addiction and mental illness, from the Broadway revue *Puzzles of 1925*, featuring a scene set in a sanitarium walled in by a crossword grid, to the song "Since Ma's Gone Crazy over Cross Word Puzzles":

The house has gone to ruin,
Since all that Mother's doin'
Is putting letters in the little squares,
We live on canned tomatoes,
And old cold boiled potatoes,
No wonder when he comes home
Father swears . . .

More than three-quarters of a century later, independent filmmaker Amir Naderi pursued the same idea when he made *Marathon*, a small film about a young woman who becomes unhinged while compulsively attempting to break her record for solving as many crosswords as she can in one day while riding the New York City subway system.

We use these terms—*compulsion, addiction, craze*—as lighthearted metaphors. But artists are always first to the game of identifying spiritual truths later confirmed by science. It will come as no surprise when brain researchers finally decide that a better understanding of why we are drawn to crosswords is in fact essential to curing mental illness.

The British Invasion

I have become bored with the crossword.

It was bound to happen, doing the *New York Times* puzzle six days a week, even on Mondays and Tuesdays. (To be honest, it's always been hard to bother with the crossword in the Sunday magazine, which—its difficulty level the same as a Wednesday or Thursday yet its size so much bigger—has always felt more like work than fun.)

It's not that I'm a genius. As with any exercise, if you work the same muscle long enough, you master the task. If you do the crossword every day for a year, you will also develop the same reflexive hyperawareness of the otherwise forgotten ERNO Rubik, POLA Negri, or Leon URIS and his protagonist ARI.

I started to look forward to the diagramless crossword, which appears periodically in the *Times* magazine below the regular crossword. It's like parachuting into the desert without a compass and finding your way home, all at your kitchen table. It requires an inner sense of where you are, as with Bill Bradley's ability to stand in the middle of the court and throw the basketball over his shoulder into the net behind him without looking. The diagramless, as the name implies, is a crossword with the black squares removed, thus leaving you on your own to figure out where to put them in. To make up for this added challenge, the clues are generally easier than they would be in a standard crossword. Once you get the hang of it, it can be a rather routine affair, but there is an elegant beauty in the way the answers ooze from top to bottom like blood from a stab wound. It tests one's orienteering abilities and therefore satisfies the hunter-gatherer within, but only once every six weeks.

There is more frequent pleasure in the acrostic, a virtuosic tour de force served up biweekly in the *Times* magazine by the husband-and-wife team of Emily Cox and Henry Rathvon. For most of my life I paid no attention to this puzzle. It was a revelation when someone pointed out how it works, very much like that dream when you discover there's a secret annex in your house, and it's been there your whole life.

The acrostic operates on multiple levels, bringing to

mind Mr. Spock's three-dimensional chess. You begin by answering typical crossword clues. Each letter of each answer has a specific coordinate linked to one in a series of empty squares. When filled in, those squares spell out a literary quotation. That in itself is quite a feat for the constructor, to come up with satisfying words of more than three letters that can be anagrammed into a quotation. Then, to top it all off, the first letter of each answer spells out the author and the source of the quote!

As the quotation starts to emerge, it is then possible to fill in answers that may have eluded you at first. Unlike the crossword, which exists in a timeless realm, the acrostic follows an arc that does make the solver aware of time. At first it seems so difficult that you wonder if you'll ever finish it. Then, when critical mass is achieved and the quotation is evident, the final filling-in of the blank squares can seem like something of a chore. It is a shape we all recognize—rising action that builds to a climax followed by a perfunctory denouement—from classical tragedy and sex.

One Sunday, the acrostic was based on a quote by writer Sarah Vowell. I e-mailed her that morning to tell her how exciting it must have been for her, that she had received a great honor that day. She answered, "I have no idea what you're talking about." I explained to her that she should solve the acrostic and gave her instructions for how to do it. She did not reply.

I kvetched to the novelist Meg Wolitzer that with respect to crosswords, I had gone as far as I could go. Even though

Will Shortz had done so much to liven up the *Times* puzzle, it still felt like a closed universe of references that was not expanding fast enough.

Meg then pointed me to the puzzles published by the *Atlantic* and *Harper's* magazines (as well as puzzles she used to make with Jesse Green for the late, lamented *Seven Days* magazine). They're known as cryptic crosswords, and they are a British invention. The puzzles in these particular magazines involve gimmicks that at first seemed confusing and off-putting. In fact, I so resisted them that I believe Meg and I had the same conversation twice, spanning an interval of about a year. The second time, something clicked when she described how the crosswords in those magazines got her through a particularly difficult period after the birth of her first son. She and her husband, Richard, would work on them day after day, night after night, passing the puzzles back and forth. It's what kept her calm.

Rather soon after our second conversation I tackled the *Atlantic* cryptic puzzle by Cox and Rathvon. Something profound had changed since my previous attempt. Perhaps it was Meg's endorsement. Perhaps a gene had switched on—the same one that gets activated when we hit thirty and start to like Brussels sprouts and the music of Jobim. Whatever it was, something not only turned me into a lover of cryptics but also set me on the self-defeating path of evangelizing on their behalf.

Please do not mistake me for an Anglophile. The appeal of London escapes me. I do not get soft at the sound of the Oxbridge accent. The food may be getting better, but there is still a long way to go on that score.

And yet, in the 1920s, England was the birthplace of two things I hold dear: the BBC and cryptic crosswords.

I have to warn you that whenever I try to share my love of cryptic crosswords, people tend to run screaming in the other direction. Please try to resist the temptation. Instead, imagine a crossword tradition that features an additional layer of wordplay, very much of the sort employed by Lewis Carroll:

> "I'm a poor man, your Majesty," the Hatter began in a trembling voice, "and I hadn't but just begun my tea—not above a week or so—and what with the bread-and-butter getting so thin—and the twinkling of the tea—"
>
> "The twinkling of *what?*" said the King.
>
> "It *began* with the tea," the Hatter replied.
>
> "Of course twinkling begins with a T!" said the King sharply.
>
> —Lewis Carroll, *Alice's Adventures in Wonderland*

With cryptic crosswords, nothing is as it seems. If you follow a clue's apparent meaning, you will quickly become unhappy. Cryptic clues look *almost* like normal sentences, but something is a little bit off.

It is essential to understand that, in these crosswords, only *part* of the clue is the actual definition, and it can come at either the beginning or end. The rest of the clue is a set of coded instructions on how to derive the answer, using one of a limited set of procedures: anagram, reversing letters, inserting one word inside another, and the like. It's up to you to figure out what's going on beneath the deliberately misleading surface meaning.

If you're thinking "WTF?" don't worry. Everyone does

at first. But if you bear with me for a moment here, there's a chance you might feel I've opened your eyes to a deeply gratifying pursuit.

Here's an example of a clue taken at random from a cryptic crossword by Cox and Rathvon: "Counterpart to pope is reformed."

Remember to ignore what the words appear to mean, and that only part of the clue is the actual definition. The rest is the cryptic part.

After you've done these awhile, you'll recognize "reformed" right away as a cryptic signifier. Here, the clue is telling you to take three words—*to pope is*—and to "re-form" them, i.e., rearrange their order. In so doing, you arrive at OPPOSITE, which is one synonym for *counterpart*.

One more essential aspect to cryptic clues: there can be no extraneous words. It is tempting to add an indefinite and definite article to smooth out the edges, making the sentence: "A counterpart to the pope is reformed." This is impermissible, because *A* and *the* cannot be parsed according to the syntax of the clue's cryptic meaning. This is the reason why, as blogger Jed Hartman put it, "The best cryptic-crossword clues read like headlines from a slightly deranged tabloid."

This kind of wordplay is especially unnerving to American solvers who got used to the *New York Times* crossword when Eugene T. Maleska was its editor. There is indeed something dangerous, subversive, transgressive about cryptic crosswords, and that's what makes them so profoundly liberating. Perhaps it helps if you enjoy literal humor, which I do, even though a psychiatrist friend informs me that this is a trait I share with schizophrenics. Knowing that literal thinking is a hallmark of autism

spectrum disorders nags at me; cryptics do an even better job than American-style crosswords of satisfying my
inner Asperger. It has become too fashionable, however,
to claim this diagnosis these days, so I'll continue to look
at things positively: the cryptic way of thinking forces you
to disengage the clutch in your brain and enter into a free-
associative state that Buddhists call *wild mind.*

In England, there is a competitive element to solving
crosswords that is different from how we do it in America.
Here, crossword tournaments reward speed, even though
solving in public, with the clock ticking, is antithetical to
the typical crossword experience. Even Will Shortz has
acknowledged as much. "There's a contradiction in the
tournament as is, because crosswords are an inherently
solitary activity," he said to me. "Why would you go to a
hotel and solve crosswords by yourself with five hundred
other people? It's crazy."

Here's one example of another way, at the English
magazine the *Observer.* The very challenging weekly puzzle at that magazine has been "set" by Jonathan Crowther
since 1972. (In the Commonwealth countries, crosswords
are created by "setters" or "compilers.") Crowther is only
the third person to hold the job since the *Observer* puzzle
first appeared in 1926. First there was Edward Powys
Mathers, who started the cryptic tradition and maybe
even wrote the first cryptic clues. Befitting his reputation as an unfair torturer, Mathers used the pseudonym
Torquemada, after Spain's first and most famous inquisitor general.

He was succeeded by D. S. Macnutt. Although Macnutt

took the name of another inquisitor, Ximenes (pronounced ZIM-e-neez in Britain), he is known for codifying the rules and insisting on fairness. Crowther, his successor, chose the name Azed, which is a reversal of Spain's second inquisitor general, Diego Deza. By spelling Deza backward, Crowther also evokes the alphabet, which, in the United Kingdom, goes from A to Zed.

Each month, Crowther, aka Azed, publishes a puzzle in which one answer is left unclued. It is up to the solver to write a clue of his or her own and send it in. Crowther then chooses the most elegant submission, writes up why he thinks it's a winner, and mails it in his monthly "slip"— a small newsletter—to subscribers. It is a reward system based on wit rather than speed.

Devotees of this puzzle know each other through the slip, and that is how Inspector Morse got his name. Morse, a police detective who is always mulling a clue while solving crimes, is known to fans in the English-speaking world through a series of books and TV dramas, which have aired in the United States on public television. He was created by Colin Dexter, one of the top solvers of the Azed puzzle. The inspector's name is an homage to Sir Jeremy Morse, who also kept appearing month after month at the top of the list of winning submissions.

"We hadn't met at that time," Sir Jeremy told me in his mews house in Kensington. "I don't think so. We might have been at a crossword dinner in the same room, but we didn't know each other. We know each other very well now. And then he made his assistant Sergeant Lewis—he took the name of a woman solver. So, it was nothing to do with the personality, and indeed Inspector Morse is a mirror image of Colin Dexter, not of me."

Sir Jeremy had greeted me at the door in a coat and

tie. He invited me to lunch—lamb, prepared by his wife and carved on the sideboard by him. He is a somewhat famous person in England, having served as head of the University of Bristol and also Lloyds Bank. He is not especially well known as the namesake of the famous inspector but does find it useful when offering tips on how to say his name—much more useful than saying "as in Morse code."

"Because of the way we don't pronounce our *R*s in England"—Morse's own *R*s, in particular, verge on *W*s— "people don't really know whether my name is Morse or Morris or what it is. Nobody knows about Morse code now, but we can always say 'As in Inspector Morse.' And sometimes they say to me 'Oh! I bet he was named after you,' you know, ironically. I just let that pass. It's complicated, you see, because I described to you the way it happened. He wasn't named after *me* as a person." And then, with a joyful, emphatic peroration straight out of an England that is fast vanishing, "He just. Has. *My. Name.* That's all there is to it."

It is easy to imagine what Colin Dexter was like as a schoolmaster, in classics. Upon meeting me, he started quizzing me with cryptic clues: "Heroic Greek crossword composed by Ximenes and Torquemada jointly."

The clue is telling you to find the word that crosses the end of Ximenes and the start of Torquemada. It doesn't seem especially elegant to me, but I was lucky, since my meeting with Dexter happened soon after I read the Robert Fagles translation of Homer's *Odyssey*, and NESTOR was still fresh in my mind.

"I'm glad you've heard of him. Well goodness me."

I quickly disappointed Dexter, though, by not knowing that the river that runs through Cambridge is the CAM.

We were in Dexter's hometown, Oxford, in the living room of Don Manley, whom Jeremy Morse described as the Will Shortz of England. Manley sets crosswords for a living and also writes books about them and, as Dexter put it, is blazingly fast at solving them, having once finished all the daily puzzles on a single train ride from Oxford to London. The trip takes about an hour. Manley is also a regular at the top of the Azed slip.

As the two men talked, they quoted memorable clues as if they were lines of poetry. I pointed out that such a thing is impossible in America, given that our puzzles are, as the two men said with a tone of slight contempt, "merely definitional."

"One remembers wonderfully clever clues," Dexter said. "This is why, with sudoku"—he pronounced it "soo-DOCK-oo"—"you don't say I saw a wonderful line this morning: six-four-three-nine."

"Don't talk to me about soo-DOCK-oo," Manley said.

I found myself feeling jealous of this crossword culture that demanded creativity from solvers, with dinners for the Azed regulars and even more frequent lunch gatherings among devotees who call themselves the Gruntlings and who trade clues back and forth. But Manley and Dexter made it clear they were describing a world that, like Jeremy Morse's plummy accent, was evaporating.

"The Azed competition is in decline," Manley said. "There's no doubt about that. It is in decline."

Dexter went on, "I think he almost had nine hundred entries at one time."

"He had one hundred seventy for the last one," Manley said.

Crowther himself had recently lamented in his monthly slip that his previous puzzle brought in only 207 entries, which he called a "disappointingly low number" for what he thought would be an easy puzzle.

The irony here is that while the British audience leaves cryptics for more straightforward puzzles, including soo-DOCK-oo, the New Wave of constructors in America, with Will Shortz at the vanguard, has helped introduce British-style wordplay and misdirection to our once "merely definitional" crosswords.

More than once I have asked Shortz to bang the drum on behalf of the cryptic crossword in America. More than once he answered, "It's not gonna happen. It's too elite."

Elite? It doesn't seem that way to me, so I asked him why.

"Because they're so hard to solve. You can't think literally. There are people who don't even like tricky crossword clues."

It is true that I once came across a woman who waited outside the Triplex movie theater in Great Barrington to ambush Shortz, because she had heard he would make an appearance in connection with the premiere of the film *Wordplay*. She wanted to give him a piece of her mind for not following "the rules," such as indicating when an answer would be an abbreviation—rules that went out the window years ago.

I disagree with Shortz's assertion that cryptics are hard because they don't let you think literally. It's just the opposite. They are easier because they don't require special knowledge as much as a willingness to think *hyperliterally*.

I'm not even sure what he means when he says cryptics are "elite." In any case, the outcome of the 2008 presidential election suggests that not everyone considers it a term of opprobrium. It did seem odd that he was so convinced they would never succeed in America. I reminded him that he had once said the same thing about number puzzles, and soon his income from sudoku books dwarfed his *Times* salary. Shortz doesn't even make those sudoku puzzles, it's just that his name carries such a tremendous amount of brand credibility. If anyone can get America to embrace cryptic crosswords, he can.

"It's not gonna happen."

Shortz did let on that when the *Wall Street Journal* started printing crosswords on Fridays, he suggested they run a good, easy, American-style cryptic. "I thought that would be classy." Now that the *Journal* is owned by Rupert Murdoch, it doesn't seem out of the question. After all, in the *New York Post*, on the same page as what the Brits call a "quick" (i.e., American-style) crossword, Murdoch reprints the cryptic puzzle from his London *Times*. This is baffling. The percentage of his American readership that can finish a cryptic made in the United Kingdom, dependent on a knowledge of British idiom and the rules of cricket, is too small to measure.

As my father would say to me on multiple occasions throughout my childhood: "If you want something done right, do it yourself." I am not ready to hand America over completely to the Know Nothings. If this means I'll have to run the cryptic crusade without Will Shortz, so be it. Maybe I can get Murdoch on board.

Don Manley and I went off to lunch at the Trout Inn, which has turned one room into a shrine to Colin Dexter and to his fictional creation, who frequented the pub. Manley did not say that cryptics could never take America by storm, but he did end up expressing the flip side of that sentiment.

"I think the fact that cryptic crosswords started in this country says something about Britishness. We're very good at starting playful things. The British are a playful people, so where these things live on, this spirit of playfulness lives on, doesn't it? You can see a strand of Britishness in cricket. You can see a strand of Britishness in rugby football. You can see a strand of Britishness in crosswords. We've given to the world a lot of recreational activities."

I asked him then if he thought it is logical that Arthur Wynne, who worked in New York but was originally from Liverpool, would have invented—

Manley interrupted, "Sure it is! I don't think any of your lot would have!"

Here is my theory of why we might be drawn to cryptic crosswords: they force you to treat words, and therefore the world, with skepticism. The underlying message of the cryptic crossword is that yes, you were right, the world is out to deceive you. It is your duty as a citizen to maintain the alarm that should sound whenever a Linda Tripp says she "found herself in a situation not of her own making," or a Charles Osgood declares on national radio, long after the facts showed otherwise, that George W. Bush won the 2000 election "fair and square."

Words lie. If the crossword does have a practical value beyond the artistic, then it is in the daily insistence on the precision of language. It is part of our training if we are to win the war on words that government waged in the first part of the twenty-first century. The hope, as articulated by George Orwell, is that if we remain alert to the special qualities of words and allow ourselves to think sideways, we might eventually demand accountability from our leaders. We settle, then, for baby steps: to see past the deceptions of words. Merely definitional crosswords protect us from the harmful words we hurl at ourselves. Cryptic puzzles hone the skills we need to decipher the lies delivered to us by the world.

Kind of a Bunch of Hooey

At least according to Francis.

What do you mean? I asked.

"I just don't agree with you. I don't think cryptic crosswords are going to help you with the world. I don't know, I just think they're two completely different things. The lies the world hurls at you and the deception of a cryptic crossword—cryptic crosswords are lying to you for fun! We all like playing with words. It's outside of the world. It is even less relatable to day-to-day experience than a crossword, because at least crosswords talk about facts which come up. Being the sort of person who'll look at a U-Haul truck and nudge the person next to me and say, 'Hey, if you delete the *H* from that and spell it backward it spells LUAU'—that just *kills* conversation. Just stops it dead. I'm here to tell you, the things you find out in cryptic crosswords are not useful in real life."

Of course.

But.

I think Francis's strong reaction comes from the fact that he makes crosswords. It must seem to him that I am implying that cryptic constructors somehow intend to vaccinate the citizenry with protective verbal armor, and that solvers consciously choose cryptic crosswords as part of their training against the cynical misuse of language. That is not what I meant at all. Every day we engage in activities in which the net result is far greater than our intentions. Worms, when they eat, give no thought to how important they are to the aeration of the soil and therefore to the human food supply.

I didn't share this analogy with Francis, worrying that he might think I was calling him a worm. Besides, I couldn't speak for constructors. I could only try to describe the feeling that goes along with solving a cryptic crossword. I let it drop. He had a puzzle to make.

We looked at his effort so far. He had started working on some ideas before I arrived. This was contrary to the purpose of our day, which was for me to observe the construction of a puzzle from beginning to end.

At that moment, an idea came to me that seemed so nuts I almost didn't say it out loud. But. What if—I knew this sounded crazy, but—what if Francis made a cryptic crossword?

"You want a cryptic? I can write you a cryptic."

I gave it careful thought. After all, we all pretty much know how a traditional, definitional crossword is made. But this new idea held out the promise of a great adventure.

Francis needed little persuading. "Cryptics are *fun*." In his tone I heard him clearly trying to push us in that direction. Once the idea was in the air, the thought of making a standard crossword seemed terribly blah. "Want me to write you a cryptic? I could do that."

And so it was decided.

Enigma

It had come to this. In the summer of 1941, British intelligence learned of unfathomable crimes perpetrated by German troops in the newly invaded Soviet Union. As the summer wore on, code breakers deciphered reports of the slaughter of many thousands of Jews. By the beginning of August, 7,819 were dead in Minsk; by the end of the month, 12,361 in the Ukraine. In the face of this new knowledge—a pattern of mass murder that had not yet been named the Holocaust— the British Empire was now pinning its hopes for the future on word nerds.

An ad hoc crew of several hundred novice cryptanalysts was assembled at the Bletchley Park estate north of London. There was no way to keep up with the increasing flow of intercepts coming in. More bodies were needed.

To recruit them, MI8, a branch of the military intelligence service, turned to the *Daily Telegraph*, which in 1925 had become the first newspaper in England to publish a crossword each day. Since the activities at Bletchley were among the best-kept secrets in the history of warfare, a subterfuge had to be devised.

Stanley Sedgewick, a clerk in a London accounting firm, was among the twenty-five or thirty readers who responded to an invitation from the newspaper's editor to enter a competition. Sedgewick told the BBC that "a Mr. Gavin, Chairman of the Eccentrics Club, wrote saying he would donate £100 to the Minesweepers' Fund if it could be demonstrated under controlled conditions that anyone could solve the *Daily Telegraph* puzzle in less than twelve minutes."

Four of the entrants succeeded in the task. Sedgewick was not among them. He had filled in all but one of the words when the bell rang. Still, he received a summons to meet with the head of MI8. "I think I was told, though not so primitively, that chaps with twisted brains like mine might be suitable for a particular type of work as a contribution to the war effort."

The *Telegraph* puzzle competition yielded five new recruits. Because of the ultra-secret nature of the operation at Bletchley, Sedgewick did not find out until long after the war was over that he had participated in cracking the German Enigma codes—a decisive factor in the Allied victory.

Don't Ask . . .

America was introduced to cryptic crosswords in the pages of the *Nation*, in 1943. Four years later, Frank W. Lewis became the magazine's sole puzzle contributor and remained so for more than six decades. His contact at the *Nation* told me Lewis had five years of puzzles stockpiled and could be dead for a long time before anyone realized it. From his biography: "Although trained as a musician, Mr. Lewis worked for thirty years as a cryptanalyst for the War Department and the National Security Agency. Much of his work is still classified."

... Don't Tell

Audrey Mantey needed to buy bread for the lunch program at the charter school where she teaches, in suburban Detroit. Taciturn, and wearing cargo pants, she got into her black Saturn SUV with its bumper sticker that read IRAQ VETERANS AGAINST THE WAR, and drove out of her way to a market owned by Iraqis.

"Shopping there is like doing penance for Desert Storm," she said.

Audrey surprised everyone who knew her in college when she left for the Defense Language Institute in Monterey, California, and started her career in military intelligence. As an undergraduate, she was a paradigmatic student at Simon's Rock in Great Barrington, Massachusetts, which, at the time, was still a hippie college with an enrollment below three hundred and a preponderance of clove cigarettes and India-print skirts long after they had vanished from the real world.

I knew her then as Audrey Rosen, and I thought it was deeply cool that her father, Mel, was a famous crossword constructor whose name I recognized. When I got in touch with Audrey again, twenty-five years after graduation, she told me that my perception and her reality could not have been further apart. Crossword puzzles, it turned out, were the bane of her childhood.

"Growing up in that scene," she said, "was completely traumatizing for me."

Before this goes any further you must understand that when I met Audrey's parents, they projected warmth instantly, and puzzlers who have known them for years corroborated their reputation as supremely kind and friendly people. From Audrey's point of view, though, their love and enthusiasm for puzzles and games—trivia in particular—had unintended and unwelcome consequences.

"When I was really small—elementary school small—there were times around the dinner table that it was a family affair to come up with lame puns around a given theme of Dad's choosing. That was fun. I have good memories of that, and of being on vacation at the beach, with Dad stretched out in the sand with graph paper, pencils, and a dictionary, composing. But once I got into the teens, they regularly wanted to play family trivia games, and I hated that with a passion. At fifteen I couldn't answer questions about TV shows that were on in the sixties, or music that was popular when my parents were young, or political figures or actors from twenty years ago. It wears you down after a while, having to answer 'I don't know'; 'I don't know that one either'; 'Sorry, never heard of them.'"

Audrey described a recurring pattern to their regular phone check-ins that continued into her adulthood. If she pleaded, "Don't ask me that," they would push back and say, "Just guess."

She'd try to hold her ground. "No, I don't want to guess." But it did no good.

"No, really. Guess. Guess! The worst that can happen is you pick the wrong answer."

"Don't make me guess. I don't want to."

And so it went.

"It's so stupid," Audrey said. "It's like taking SATs every damn week. I'm not sure how to describe how frustrating that was—and still is at times. Once they start playing quiz show at me, I shut down. I know they view it as a test of intelligence, and I suppose it is a valid test of intelligence, but the result is that if I don't know an answer, and then the next answer, and the one after that, I feel stupid. There were times I just wanted a tattoo on my forehead that said 'inadequate' so we could be done with it. As an adult, I've gone to a couple of puzzle conventions with my parents so that we could vacation together—but it's always with the prenegotiated understanding that I will not be participating in any of the games, under any circumstances. And once we get there, they always try to change my mind, and they're insulted that I don't want to take part in this thing that is such a huge part of their lives."

I suggested that instead of going to puzzle conventions she should start an organization of her own: Adult Children of Crossword Constructors. She seemed intrigued by the idea.

"Maybe my parents would finally get the hint. 'No! Don't make me answer it!' isn't as direct as one might think."

A tremendous irony hung over our conversations, and it had nothing to do with reconciling her admiration for Lenin with her participation in the effort to bring down the Soviet Union. Even more striking: Audrey felt traumatized by her upbringing around puzzles, and yet she spent most of her adult years working in cryptanalysis. She recognized that crosswords and crypto come from the same place, but didn't see the paradox until we started talking. It turned out that despite her feelings of inadequacy, Audrey did quite well in her field.

"The test to be a linguist in the army starts out with a pair of headphones, a pencil, and an answer sheet. Over the course of the exam, they teach you a made-up language. You learn how to recognize a verb in the language, a noun, some vocabulary. An hour or so into it, you have to identify which sentences are grammatically correct in this nonexistent language. Partway through that test, I gave up in frustration. I laid the pencil down and just sat there, stumped, unable to continue. Then I realized that the recruitment people weren't going to let me leave the room halfway through their test, so I picked the pencil back up and resumed filling in answer bubbles, purely out of boredom. I was convinced I'd failed it. Even with the section I didn't complete, I scored great on the test, one of the higher scores my recruiter had seen."

Once admitted into army intelligence, Audrey's technical training included something known as the Electronic Warfare Signals Intelligence Course.

"A typical exam would be a huge stack of papers thrown down in front of us, all written in gibberish, and the instructor would say, 'You have two hours.' At the start of those exams, I'd know nothing. There was always a point in the process where I knew I would never be able to make any sense of anything on those papers. By the end, though, I could tell you all about their communication nets, what type of units were communicating, the nationality of the Morse operators, etc. I kicked ass at that."

Most 12-step slogans I've heard in my life have reinforced my desire never to have anything to do with the Program. There is one, however, that rings so true I repeat it whenever I can, and it is this: Feelings Aren't Facts. Audrey embodied this truth writ large. One's self-image of inadequacy, particularly when it comes to intelligence, often has nothing to do with reality. I've lost count of my friendships and romances with people who thought they were not smart enough to solve crossword puzzles. As for my attempts to show them otherwise—to put forth, first and foremost, that *of course* they were smart and, second, that crosswords really don't require intelligence, anyway— well, I had about as much success as Audrey's parents.

In Audrey's case, it seemed she did in fact love trivia— about one particular subject.

"I loved knowing trivia about Morse code abbreviations. I began to teach myself small bits of Morse code and practiced it in secret. I passed notes to my friends written in dots and lines, and forced them to decode my messages. I loved the course, and I idolized the guys at Bletchley Park who worked on cracking the Enigma. Even now, twenty years later, whenever they run a movie or a show about the Enigma on television, I have to watch it. If it comes up in conversation, if I hear someone randomly mention it, my heart skips a beat. I have an emotional attachment to that piece of machinery that really makes no sense; I have a schoolgirl crush on a scrap of metal. They say women who have a history of being abused continue to be drawn to abusive relationships. That's how the Enigma is to me, it's the ultimate bad guy; there is something completely mysterious and dark and unobtainable about that machine that makes it irresistible to me."

Audrey is politically engaged. I visited her soon after she returned from marching through the Gulf Coast in the wake of Hurricane Katrina. And she makes art—dream-like art, often using computer-manipulated photographs, occasionally with text that is incomprehensible. For her, one of the overriding themes of her work is the inaccessibility of language, which she sees as an expected response to her childhood (and adulthood) spent struggling with her parents over puzzles and trivia games.

There has been some progress on that score. She warmed up to crossword puzzles for a time when she was pregnant, a fact that reminded me instantly of Meg Wolitzer's story and made me wonder if there is not some marketing opportunity to be pursued.

"But I still freeze with primordial fear when my parents start relaying their favorite trivia questions to me over the phone: 'Go on, guess the answer. Just GUESS.'"

Audrey reported improvement in that realm as well, saying that her father finally started to grasp that when she says she doesn't want to be quizzed, she means it.

"He knows that my anxiety level just spikes way out of control with that. There've definitely been times my mom started doing the trivia quiz thing, giving me multiple choice questions, and my dad has stepped in and given her a swift kick under the table and told her to knock it off. When you look at it like that it's funny."

Despite her regular and ongoing self-examination, the crossword continued to exert an influence on Audrey that she didn't understand. There was a moment when she said it was the inherent superficiality of crossword puzzles that made her rebel—that pure intellect, without purpose, made her uncomfortable. But after she gave it more thought, she realized this analysis didn't stand up to scrutiny.

"Even though the crypto stuff is being used for the military, which I guess I'm opposed to, it was purposeful and in that sense, a little better than not a good purpose." Within a moment, though, she changed her mind. "Maybe the superficial is better than that, eh? I don't know how good it is to have a sense of purpose when you don't like the purpose."

People with lesser minds might be tempted to take

a statement such as this and label Audrey a flip-flopper. Instead, I think of F. Scott Fitzgerald's remark: "The test of a first-rate intelligence is the ability to hold two opposing ideas in mind at the same time and still retain the ability to function." I do know from my own experience that such willingness to test every idea to its limit is one surefire way to succeed at solving crossword puzzles.

La Divina Commedia, with Peacock Obbligato

If it seems disappointing that scientists have not tried to understand why humans are drawn to crosswords, it's downright odd that they still have no solid understanding of why humans make music. Until they come up with one, I'm sticking to mine: like the crossword, it induces time travel.

One July, I received a welcome invitation from a musician friend to escape the city (high heat and humidity forecast the whole week) and hang out as a guest for a few days at the Marlboro Music Festival in Vermont, where the presence of America's chamber music royalty in the mid-twentieth century—Rudolf Serkin, Pablo Casals, and the Budapest String Quartet—is still felt in the practice rooms.

How anyone can practice amid the noise is beyond me. At one point in Marlboro College's history, someone brought with him a population of peacocks. They have stayed. The afternoon I arrived, I was transfixed by the sound of a violinist in a dorm room working on the last movement of Beethoven's Opus 132 string quartet, perhaps my favorite piece of music ever in the whole history of ever. (No matter how many recordings I buy of this piece, the first performance I ever encountered, by the Yale Quartet, is what keeps returning to my iPod.) I listened to this 25 percent performance of the quartet, filling in the other three parts in my mind, transported to that melancholy yet defiant place in the soul that only Beethoven understands, when suddenly—*caw!*

How presumptuous of me to sneak into one of those practice rooms to play through "Solace," by Scott Joplin, the only piece of music I have ever committed to memory. That happened when I was in college. Sitting at a Steinway on a small campus roughly the same size and with the same woody feel as the one I attended, I was sucked through a ripple in the fabric of space-time to the Steinway in Blodgett House. It was 1984, the year after I graduated and also, as it happens, smack dab in the middle of the road of my life so far.

By that time, I had already realized I would not have a career as a professional musician, for reasons I'm reminded of today. That knotty chromatic passage in the B section I always struggled with? I still do. Why? Because I still gloss over it, decades later, so I can enjoy the luscious parts toward the end that come more easily. Hearing that violinist in the next studio at Marlboro, who repeats the same two measures of Beethoven over and over and over and over and over and over and over and over again, I am forced to confront what true discipline is.

On that day half a lifetime ago, I had also realized I would not be marrying the woman to whom I was engaged. Calling her a woman seems funny now, as funny as the thought that we were planning to marry while we were both still children. I'm sure she's as thankful as I am that we didn't go through with it. There she was at the far end of the room while I played, and she was crying. It had nothing to do with the quality of my performance. It was Scott Joplin who made her cry, because "Solace" provides anything but. It will dislodge any repressed pain and force it from your body, through your tear ducts when necessary. This piece had been with us for years, reminding us now of the good times and making it clear once and for all that they would not be coming back.

I would like to be able to say it was my playing that spoke to her, but I was neither good enough nor bad enough to move anyone to tears. As a musician, I've always been controlled by thought rather than feeling, and this was the real deal-breaker standing in the way of a musical career. It's not something I like to do often, but I can ride that wrinkle in time back even further to a recital my sophomore year, to that same Steinway grand. My plan was to make it through a note-perfect account of Mozart's Fantasia in D Minor. If I could do that, I would consider the evening a success. There was never any chance the performance would become more than just a series of notes and take flight as an expression of something human, but I was willing to live with that trade-off. Had to, thanks to a paralyzing fear of making mistakes in public. And so I approached musical scores as if they were crosswords. As I started the last line of the score, I was overjoyed. Not a single note wrong! Congratulations were premature, though. In letting myself get distracted from the task at hand, which required every bit of concentration I had, I brought about the one thing that scared me to death. The final cadence came out as if it had been rewritten by Schoenberg—a clangorous, atonal joke. According to a friend who was there, I greeted the polite applause with a vacant look of shock on my face. That was the moment I stopped considering a life in music.

Today when I run through "Solace," it is a disaster. It's going to take some work to get the notes back, especially in the B section. I decide instead to go at it differently. For the rest of the session, the goal is to ignore technical problems and play the piece in a way that has the potential to move me to tears. I try to hear the music as a listener while I play, which in the past has always seemed impossible. I take it slowly, remembering something the jazz bassist Charlie Haden once said about playing every note as if your life depended on it. I make many mistakes, and so I take it once more, with feeling. What's to be afraid of? There's no one else listening, save the peacocks.

Tradition and the Individual Talent

It seems odd that when people want to understand a creative work, they often begin by learning something about its creator. I may have been too influenced by T. S. Eliot's assertion that biography should have nothing to do with appreciating a work of art. (Of course, he was highly motivated to steer people away from inquiring about unflattering details of his personal life.) It seems all too easy to forget that works of art—music in particular—result from a great deal of effort exerted by a living, human imagination. They often seem to have sprung up from a well in the ground.

Will Shortz made it hard to hold on to this illusion when he started attaching bylines to the daily puzzles in the *Times*. Suddenly, the solver was faced with the various quirks of personality associated with this or that constructor.

After I noticed how much I admired the puzzles of Michael Shteyman and started digging into his background, I couldn't help but wonder if he deliberately sprinkled autobiographical statements into his clues. Shteyman's story is noteworthy. He immigrated to Baltimore from Saint Petersburg at the age of twelve, graduated early from Johns Hopkins, and continued to play the piano and compose while working in a neuroscience lab studying glutamine receptors, which are implicated in learning and memory, and analyzing how phosphorylation of the glutamine receptors influences other proteins. When he was barely in his twenties he had already contributed more than twenty-five puzzles to the *New York Times*.

It had to have been a conscious choice to include, all in one themeless puzzle: "Language study topic" (TENSE), "Dictionary features" (USAGENOTES), "Not native" (ALIEN), and "Duma demurral" (NYET). And then there was "Advanced missile feature" (HEATSENSOR), which, although less direct, does point to one of the facts of life that for years cast a shadow over both his home and adopted countries.

Marc Romano, in *Crossworld*, also noted how Shteyman tends to insert biographical details into his puzzles. Romano and I have come to different conclusions, however, about the constructor's prowess with words. Romano considers it "amazing" that Shteyman makes exceptional puzzles in English. I wonder if creating in a second language is less a handicap and in some way a leg up. Think of his fellow Russian émigrés Vladimir Nabokov and musical lexicographer Nicolas Slonimsky, who both approached the English tongue with ears so unprejudiced that their prose seemed incapable of cliché. Still, although Shteyman's otherness may have attuned him to special qualities of English words, it turns out his struggles with the language section in his standardized tests delayed his entry into medical school. He is so gifted, it seems quite possible he could someday discover the neural circumstance that makes such a paradox possible.

You Don't Gotta Have a Gimmick

The reason cryptics are not popular in America has nothing to do with elitism. It has to do with presentation.

The cryptic puzzles in the *Atlantic* used to come with a caveat: "It is assumed you know how to decipher clues." There is no way a newcomer could know such a thing! In the pre-Internet world, readers were invited to write in for an explanation to be sent in the mail. Nowadays, the *Atlantic* puzzles are accompanied by a link that takes you to an explanation of how cryptics work, a definite improvement. But when cryptic crosswords appear in *Harper's* and the *New York Times*, they come with zero warnings that different rules apply. How could a first-time solver possibly have any idea of what to do?

All it takes is a little hand-holding. I envision a slightly more useful text than what the *Atlantic* offered. Because space is so tight, it must be concise, something like: "Ignore surface meanings. Clues must be deciphered." That's more specific, and one word shorter.

Francis stared at the computer screen and considered what style of cryptic to make. He immediately ruled out an *Atlantic*- or *Harper's*-style crossword, which, in my view, have never taken off in the United States because they involve another layer of complication. Known as "variety cryptics" and descended from the puzzles that appeared in the BBC's *Listener* magazine, these puzzles require you, for example, to delete letters before entering them into the grid, or else to apply the rules of football, or some other nonsense. These gimmicks are meant to increase interest. For me, they have the opposite effect. They're downright annoying, in fact.

The cryptic crossword, if it is to find an audience in America, should be modeled on the London *Times* puzzle. The Cartesian purity of these grids, known as black-square or block puzzles, gives them a much better chance of achieving gateway-drug status.

Francis called up a blank, black-square cryptic grid and stared at the screen some more, during which time, in various places around the world, grass grew longer and paint became dry.

On Curation

People ask what impact computers will have on crossword puzzles. Invariably they wonder about the construction of grids, as if using a program somehow constitutes cheating.

The more important worry about the computer has to do with the ready availability of knowledge. It is simply too easy now to google your way through a crossword, and that's reflected in some puzzles. More and more we have off-loaded the storage and retrieval of facts onto remote computer servers, accessible by devices that we now literally keep in our pockets.

"A question I am asked often is this: 'Is it cheating to use references?'" Will Shortz once wrote. "In reply I always quote Will Weng, one of my predecessors as *Times* crossword editor: 'It's your puzzle. Solve it any way you want.'"

I won't claim never to have looked for answers online, but it does feel dirty, like paying for sex.

The editors of newspaper crosswords attempting to rival the *New York Times*—Peter Gordon, former editor of the *Sun*, and Stanley Newman of *Newsday*—have both said to me that they make puzzles using facts they looked up on the Internet. By contrast, I have heard Will Shortz say more than once, with regard to a piece of obscure knowledge he has rejected, "I don't think most people would know that."

This goes a long way toward explaining the superiority of the *Times* crossword. Will Shortz sees himself as a curator of America's cultural literacy. The assumption is that, as educated citizens, we keep a body of information in our heads: some of it falls into the category of general knowledge; the rest is trivia. Shortz says this is where he differs from fellow editors such as Stanley Newman.

"One little thing I don't care for about his puzzles," Shortz said, "is that a big way for him to make a puzzle hard is to be obscure—to throw in some trivia people won't know. I don't find that personally satisfying and I don't think solvers as a whole like that. They would rather have their minds teased and tugged at. I always want people to understand the answer once they get it, and I don't think that's always true of his, and I know it's not true of Peter Gordon's. His puzzles are very hard and they're even harder than the *Times*'s. He does very good puzzles and he has lots of clever clues, but he has a lot more obscure trivia and names in his puzzles. If that were done in the *Times*, it would not be popular."

For me, the ready accessibility of information renders the crossword obsolete—at least the crossword as we know it in America, the kind that depends on mere definitions. Keeping vast amounts of knowledge in our heads is simply no longer necessary, and that creates a need for puzzles that can't be solved with the help of Google. Maybe this is why sudoku has become so popular. It certainly buttresses my case for cultivating a market for cryptic crosswords on these shores.

Then there is the matter of deciding what counts as general knowledge.

"There are people who don't like me," Shortz said. "I know they would *hate* Peter, because he goes even further than I do. They don't know modern culture. They don't read the newspaper. They don't go to movies. They don't know slang. They apparently don't know young people. There's a lot of stuff I put in the puzzles that I think is part of being culturally literate that they don't think is part of cultural literacy. I think some people just want puzzles to stick in the period when they first did them."

Those of us not in this category solve puzzles partly to reassure ourselves that we are staying current. But current with what standard? While Gordon's puzzles can be more difficult than Shortz's, they reflect the fact that he is a devoted sports fan. Shortz, by his own admission, couldn't care less about sports, and for that I am truly grateful.

In many ways Gordon and Shortz represent nonoverlapping universes. This is a reality of our time. The era when all of America watched Ed Sullivan at the same moment has vaporized into uncountable niche media markets.

Anyone who has ever wondered just exactly what crossword editors do could find out firsthand, thanks to a rare slipup. On Monday, August 22, 2005, customers who bought an actual *Times* made from paper solved a puzzle by Lynn Lempel. For a brief time, however, the online version of that day's puzzle was by someone else: Anthony J. Salvia. The problem was the *Sun* had published a version of his same puzzle four months earlier. Shortz discovered what had happened and changed puzzles before the *Times* went to press.

Amy Reynaldo, who has developed a nascent critical vocabulary in her blog Diary of a Crossword Fiend—I think of her as the Pauline Kael of crosswords—pointed out that "a whopping five out of the nine discrete zones" are different in the two versions of the puzzle. My statistical analysis confirms her findings.

The theme entries are the same. The central entry, CANES, defines the theme, a set of homophones: CAINEMUTINY, KEYBISCAYNE, CAINANDABEL, CITIZENKANE.

That's just about the only place where the puzzles show any similarity. Out of a total of seventy-six answers, forty are different. That's almost 53 percent.

That leaves thirty-six answers that are the same in both versions of the puzzle. Only eight of those clues are identical in both puzzles—presumably, as Salvia wrote them. Nineteen of the clues have been slightly tweaked. Nine of the clues have a different sense altogether, even though they relate to the same answers.

In some ways, the editors were true to form. Mel OTT, who epitomizes the ultra-long tail of crossword celebrity, makes an appearance in Gordon's *Sun* puzzle. ABA, which Shortz clues as "Attorney's org.," is, for Gordon, a "Sports league that used a red-white-and-blue ball: Abbr." But then there are surprises. Shortz is the one who clues ANA as "'Gimme _____!' (start of an Auburn cheer)" whereas Gordon asks for it as "Santa _____ (city in California)." And Shortz, of all people, lets the hackneyed hockey legend Bobby ORR into the party.

Both editors permit crosswordese—OLIO (as in "hodgepodge") in the *Times* versus ALIA (cf. "et al.") in the *Sun*. I call it a toss-up. Gordon uses EPEE, a type of fencing sword that is so ubiquitous in crosswords that I would personally ban the word from any puzzle of mine, but it's not as if Shortz hasn't used it a bajillion times.

It's more instructive to compare the puzzles with regard to elegance. The *Times* puzzle fails once at the micro-level, allowing SAWER ("Carpenter, often"—have you ever used this word or known anyone who has?) but does a better job overall.

The answer GEN appears in Shortz's puzzle alone, permitting two clues in this puzzle to refer to each other: "Their story is told in 44-Across," which is an abbreviation for the biblical book where CAINANDABEL live. Gordon's puzzle has PEN instead of GEN, so the opportunity for a cross-reference there is lost.

ORSON appears at 1-Down in the puzzle edited by Gordon, who offers the clue: "'War of the Worlds' narrator Welles." And yet 10-Down is CITIZENKANE, crying out for someone to say, "Hey, look, there's a connection to be made here!" This comes across as inattentiveness on the editor's part.

The cluing of KEYBISCAYNE is instructive. It offers, I think, a glimpse into what sets the *Times* puzzle apart from the rest. Shortz clues it as "Nixon's Florida home" and thereby tests our general knowledge. Gordon's clue—"The Rickenbacker Causeway takes you there"—is trivia.

A More Convincing Theory from Will Shortz on Why We Solve Puzzles

"I think a big part of the appeal is that there are so few things in life—life is so complicated today—so few things you see through from start to finish. You know, you get thrown into the middle. You drive a car, but do you really understand all the workings of the car engine? I don't. When I turn on the furnace in my house and the heat starts coming out, do I really know what's going on in that furnace that's making that happen? Not really. Whereas with a crossword, you follow it through from square one to the end. And in this day and age, that's a very satisfying feeling."

It was the first time I'd ever heard anyone use *from square one* in this context. It had a new freshness to it. I wondered aloud if this was, in fact, its origin before it declined into cliché. Will Shortz told me he believed that not only is it a phrase that may have entered the language from crosswords, it might be the *only* such expression.

For the record, standard references put forth a different derivation. According to the *Oxford English Dictionary*, the term is "often said to derive from the notional division of an association football pitch into eight numbered sections for the purposes of early radio commentaries. . . . This suggestion cannot be upheld with any certainty, and the phrase may simply come from a board-game such as Snakes and Ladders."

Late to the Game

On February 15, 1942—eighteen years after deriding crosswords as "a primitive form of mental exercise"—the

New York Times changed course and started printing a Sunday crossword, one of the last major American newspapers to do so. It took another eight years for the daily puzzle to make its debut. The paper picked its first crossword editor, Margaret Petherbridge, from the troika (with Prosper Buranelli and F. Gregory Hartswick) behind the Simon & Schuster series of books. The wealth she accumulated editing crosswords helped finance the launch, in 1946, of the publishing house cofounded by her husband, John Farrar, with Roger Straus.

Letter to a Young Constructor

"Crosswords are an entertainment. Avoid things like death, disease, war and taxes—the subway solver gets enough of that in the rest of the paper."
—Margaret Petherbridge Farrar,
to sixteen-year-old novice constructor Merl Reagle

Play as You Go

"You see that this takes a while," Francis said, during one very long stretch of silence. "There's a huge difference between writing cryptics and writing a crossword."

For example, Francis did not first solidify his grid and proceed from there, which is how he would create a standard crossword puzzle. There was a constant back-and-forth between choosing his words and devising the clues. His reason for doing things this way makes complete sense: he didn't want to put in a word that would be too difficult to clue. Part of the triage in making a cryptic involves ensuring you'll have reasonable options for word-play, the essential ingredient. And that's what makes them more fun for a puzzle maker like Francis. Making this kind of puzzle is "write-y," fun. Like writing a poem.

Unlike the tedious work of coming up with fresh definitions for an ordinary crossword.

"If you're like me and you try to come up with clues that have not been used before, it can be like pulling teeth to try to find a way of approaching a clue that hasn't been done. It's a lot more research-y and that's not a thing I love. I hate it."

Odd for someone who chooses to make his living creating crossword puzzles.

The Breakfast Club

Within a twelve-month period I lost my wife and child.

I've never actually been married in the eyes of the law or God, but it was a virtual marriage—living together with the intention that it would last a lifetime—that came to an end abruptly and without warning. Technically speaking, I've never been a father, either, but for five years I was at the center of a creative enterprise, a public radio show, and creating it—building it around my sensibility, an extension of my self—was the nearest I'll ever get to giving birth. I can't presume to comprehend the unspeakable grief that accompanies the death of one's child and I hope never to know it firsthand. Of the senseless and unnecessary losses in my own life, however, the cancellation of *The Next Big Thing* tops the list.

Both episodes were traumatic, and although one can never make this kind of self-diagnosis, I have to believe that some state of shock enveloped me in a protective wrapping of numbness. I really don't know how I felt at the time. Observing my crossword habits was the only barometer I had to gauge my mental state.

In the case of the romance, it was a violent ripping apart, bigger than the mere disintegration of a partnership. I had made a strategic error, neglecting my own friendships as I inserted myself into her tribe of friends, which dropped me as hard as she did. It resulted in many weeks of sitting alone and staring at the living room wall and seeing images of fiery plane crashes, my body slowly succumbing to sixth-degree burns.

For the first time in several years, the daily crossword exited my morning routine. This may seem contradictory, given the argument I've been making about the puzzle's therapeutic benefits, but in moments of extreme trauma the crossword seems not only inadequate but also inappropriate. In the weeks and months after September 11, it felt somehow disrespectful to be working on crosswords instead of bearing witness to the dead. Then, and again after this near-marriage collapsed, I developed the habit of sleeping with the lights and the television on. It was too dangerous to risk going deep within myself. That's where the monsters resided, and anything that pushed me near them—crosswords, deep sleep—had to be suspended until I knew they were gone.

It wasn't that the dreams were bad. They were usually quite happy, a desperately needed relief. What I sought to avoid at all costs was passing through the scrim that separates the dreaming from the waking self, the emerging from a benevolent dream place and getting hit with a feeling of dread so concentrated it was unconnected to language and even to images or associations. Just a pure emotion that wordlessly communicated, *Oh no. Something really, really awful has happened. I have no idea what it is, but it must be the worst thing ever.*

This went on for a couple of months, until the end of the apartment lease forced some action on my part. The first step was to make plans to return to Manhattan. I had taken up residence in that other borough in an act of compromise, to please the militantly pro-Brooklyn virtual wife. Brooklyn always felt like the Chicago of New York: parochial, boosterish, oddly proud to be the second city within the city.

In deciding where to live next, my primary criterion was to find an apartment within walking distance of a café I used to visit before my Brooklyn exile, an inviting place with wood floors, white-painted brick and warm lighting. Some homing instinct kicked in and sent me back there. It's no coincidence that its name, Doma, is the Czech word for *home*. Doma was a ten-minute walk from my new apartment, a Greenwich Village garret, and even though it involved a substantial detour each morning before work, I stopped by the newspaper store around the corner, picked up the *New York Times*, and arrived at Doma just as the doors opened at 7:45, every morning, seven days a week. The magnetic pull emanated from the large community table in the center of the room. Since I was usually the first one there, I would take my place at the head with my back to the wall, order my coffee and something to eat, open the newspaper, and spend some time with the puzzle before heading to the office. These were the bricks I had at my disposal to build a new life.

Over the course of the next several weeks, I noticed many of the same faces starting to appear and before long, though we hadn't introduced ourselves, we would acknowledge one another's regular attendance with a good morning and sometimes a knowing grin. Beyond that our interactions never went beyond asking for the sugar. Gradually, a kind of static electricity began to build up around the table, its charge intensifying until finally the guy with the shaved head and wolflike eyes sitting to my right released it with a simple question.

"What did you get for 14-Across?"

What's remarkable and slightly magical about what happened next is that from this table, friendships were formed among people of different ages and from nonoverlapping orbits who would never have the occasion to meet one another under normal circumstances. It turned out that my fellow crossword solver was Bill, an out-of-work corporate lawyer allowing himself lots of time with several newspapers every day to plot his next move. Our de facto Breakfast Club also included Roz, a former publicist who was building a second career as a jazz singer, and JoAnne, who edited publications for a literacy foundation and was getting ready to enter graduate school in creative writing. There was B.J., a university photography teacher, and Keri, an actress everyone knew already from the TV show *Felicity*, and who, at first, we pretended not to recognize. Finally, in a walk-on role (he didn't show up every day like the rest of us) was Seth, the author of books and magazine articles we also knew because he had extensively chronicled his own history as a functioning heroin addict, and such information is the very blood that keeps café society alive.

New Yorkers like to believe that this kind of unlikely coming together from different worlds can happen only in the city where we live, but it seems municipal-centric to say so out loud. The fact is, it could happen anywhere and does. In our case, it had less to do with the city and everything to do with crosswords. I won't say the puzzle was solely responsible for breaking down the barriers, but it was a prime factor. It's possible to trace a direct line from 14-Across to the evening when Bill invited us all to his parents' apartment for a private salsa class led by a teacher whose name was Ricky Ricardo. I swear on my life that's his real name.

These episodes come and go like Brigadoon. In our case, nearly all of us were in transition of some sort, and this spontaneous Breakfast Club served its purpose until it didn't anymore. It was the crossword puzzle that told me it was time to move on. Once the lubricant for social inter-action, it had turned into a fortress wall. I found myself hiding behind it like a husband, pretending I couldn't hear B.J. scold the *New York Times* for the dispiriting news it brought each morning of the latest Bush scandals. It's not that I disagreed with her politics, it's just that they seemed obvious and loud, and at eight in the morning I try to calm my agitation rather than stir it up. Pretending I couldn't hear, I immersed myself in the grid with the hope that the nattering would go away. It didn't, and so I did. Doma is no longer at the center of my life, but several of the friendships I formed there are.

On more than one occasion I consoled myself with words along these lines: *Sure, the romance that I thought would last forever has vanished, but still I'm lucky to have my job.* Then I learned that the management of WNYC was planning to solve a station-wide financial crisis by canceling *The Next Big Thing,* and that they weren't going to tell us about it until weeks before it was to happen. Even though the show was a success, in a moment of panic selling, the president, when told by the board that she had no wiggle room to balance the upcoming year's budget, decided the most expedient solution was to jettison us. With my *Newsweek* knowledge of *The Art of War*, I understood that if I was going to save the show, I would have to think like my opponent. However, my orientation, nurtured as it is by crosswords, is still informed by a somewhat unfashionable notion of fairness, and so I was at a loss. Although we were not part of the problem, we were part of the solution.

Any remaining feelings of devastation over the loss of my romantic relationship were neatly swept aside by this news, which suddenly concentrated my mind on one thing only: save the show. I entered into warrior mode, and the puzzle reentered my daily routine as a key component of my training.

Through the Looking-Glass

Sometimes you have to go at a problem the way I go at a complicated crossword puzzle. Sometimes I picked up the Saturday *New York Times* crossword puzzle and I'd go through way over half the clues before I'll know the answer to one. And then you start with what you know the answer to and you just build on it, and eventually you can unravel the whole puzzle. And so I rarely work a puzzle of any difficulty from 1-Across and 1-Down all the way to the end in a totally logical fashion. And I think a lot of difficult, complex problems are like that. You have to find some aspect of it that you understand and build on it until you can unravel the mystery that you're trying to understand.

—Bill Clinton, in *Wordplay*

With a lot of problems, yes. But certainly not all. The truth of the president's statement once again hinges on a single word. It depends on what the definition of *sometimes* is. Some problems simply don't have any solution at all.

Connection to Loyal Center

A second thing helped snap me out of the paralysis induced by the breakup of my household. It was a phone conversation with my ex, after she had left, during which she referred to herself as homeless. Since her departure had been voluntary, it seemed especially insulting to actual homeless people, and her word choice prompted me to ask, "What was I thinking?" It was this misuse of language that allowed me to stop longing for her once and for all.

Self-pity is never flattering, so it brings me special chagrin to admit that I had moments when I entertained the possibility of my own homelessness. With the real likelihood of soon losing my income, I tried to forgive those instances when I imagined myself on the street.

And then I passed myself, sitting cross-legged on the sidewalk, immersed in a crossword puzzle—a version of myself, had I grown up in a different part of New Jersey, been born in August rather than June of 1963, and become homeless.

His name was Linkoya Boyer. His explanation of how to pronounce his last name sounded tired, rehearsed. "Like Charles Boyer."

I suggested maybe he was related. Linkoya's eyes widened, embarrassed for me because he thought I didn't realize the actor, unlike him, was white.

"Going way, way back," I said.

A laugh erupted from the bottom of his throat. "Yeah, at least six degrees of separation."

I have never seen Linkoya without a crossword puzzle.

"I started doing the puzzle when I was a kid," he told me. "My mother introduced me to it. Once I had a girlfriend who tended bar, and she used to ask me, 'What's a four-letter word for—?' I'd say, 'Gimme that!'"

Linkoya told me that each day he took money given to him by passersby and spent it on the *New York Post* and *Daily News*. I asked him if there were ever days when he had to choose between buying the newspaper and buying food.

"No. There have been days when I have to decide which will come first. I've gone without breakfast. There are days when I wake up first thing in the morning and I have just got to do the puzzle. Give me that puzzle! I've got to have it!"

I know that feeling, and so I asked Linkoya if the crossword reduces his anxiety, as it does mine.

"I don't know, don't you think it's just the opposite? When you can't get an answer? The *Post* on Saturday is hard. I remember the first time I finished, I was on top of the world. I've never had that feeling again. I've spent the whole time since trying to get that feeling back."

This is the thing about addiction. Whether the substance is narcotics, alcohol, or puzzles, what starts as a pursuit of novelty can eventually morph into a disastrous, self-defeating search for that feeling that comes when the dopamine starts flowing.

Linkoya folded the *Post* to the puzzle page and handed it to me. His eyes were filled with wonder and amazement, as if he had discovered an arcane, holy mystery.

"Do you know what to do with this?"

Did I ever. He was showing me the *other* puzzle on the page—not the "quick crossword" but the *Times* of London puzzle. I told Linkoya it would be nearly impossible for him to solve it and suggested instead he try the American-made cryptic crossword in the *Nation*. This got him excited, as if this news were opening up a new world of possibilities. "Where can I buy it? Is that a conservative paper?"

No, I said, just the opposite. Linkoya thought he had heard about it on ABC Radio, which was no doubt true, since Rush Limbaugh has been known to call the *Nation*'s editor "Hurricane" Katrina vanden Heuvel.

I bought Linkoya a book of cryptic puzzles made by Emily Cox and Henry Rathvon. I admit I was trying to hook him, but while crosswords may be as addictive as drugs or alcohol, they seemed much less likely to kill him than whatever was keeping him in his current state. There was one hitch I hadn't anticipated. The Cox and Rathvon books are branded as Mensa puzzles, a disaster for my campaign to popularize cryptic crosswords in America. He looked at the book title and then up at me.

"Are you a member of Mensa?" He seemed to be shaking.

No, I explained. You don't have to be a genius to do these puzzles. It's just that they seem difficult because, instead of testing knowledge, they challenge your problem-solving skills. It's all about letting your mind go.

When I came back to check on how he had enjoyed the gift, he let on that it had pretty much been a flop.

Several times I arranged to meet Linkoya in Union Square Park and he stood me up. One summer evening I waited about three hours and left once the mosquitoes started biting.

The next morning I happened to go by and saw him sleeping on a bench. He woke up, waved at me, and went back to sleep. I walked down the street to buy him the *Daily News* and the *Post*. When I got back he was talking with another homeless man with a sunburned complexion who had assumed the role of mayor in this particular group.

Linkoya apologized for not showing up the night before. He acknowledged he had put me out, but said he'd had "a really rough night."

What happened?

"I don't want to talk about it. It's been rough lately. But I figure you just got to stop complaining, pick yourself up, and get on with it."

Did he ever stay in the shelter?

He said that's a circle he doesn't like to travel in. "Very clique-y."

Did he need medication?

"I can feel my heart skips a beat." He touched his fingers to his wrist. "Sometimes my heart races. There's something wrong with my head. Spinning, flashes—"

How long had he been homeless?

"Let's see, I broke up with my girlfriend in nineteen ninety-eight or ninety-nine."

And that was the entirety of his answer.

"I went to community college, but the guidance counselor was fucked up. She sent me to a class on COBOL 1. I never even touched a computer. I was like, this is a computer language, and I haven't even touched a computer! That was fucked up. She was terrible."

How did he become homeless?

"Let's put it this way. Like you, I've made some poor choices in the girlfriend department. My girlfriends have been psycho. I don't know if there's any other kind, like, like—" He pointed with both index fingers, turned his long hands upright like a dancer in a Bollywood film, and laughed.

The last time I saw Linkoya was on the Fourth of July, a suitable day to consider the braid of independence and dependency that defined his life. I had recently seen the movie *Wordplay*. The imp of the perverse had made me want to take him to the New York premiere, but I didn't want to risk humiliating him. Linkoya asked about the movie, and I told him about the celebrities who appear in it, and quickly the conversation moved to Julia Roberts, who is not in the film but who, to Linkoya, looks like a horse and does not seem very talented. Then he asked me what I thought of Tom Cruise, and before I could answer, Linkoya let me know he thought Cruise was out of his mind. "He believes that stuff literally!"

Linkoya is attracted to Buddhism. He meditates, and he feels that the crossword puzzle brings on the same state of mind. "If people could do that just a few minutes a day, they'd shut the crap out of their lives."

There were two other homeless men sitting at a table nearby. One had scabs all over his face. The other, unshaven and possessing a distended stomach with a scar up its center, approached to interrupt our conversation. He pointed to a bruise and asked Linkoya if he thought he had slept on it wrong. When he came up and touched Linkoya with his shirtless belly, it was as if he wanted him to smell how much he reeked of shit.

"Go away," Linkoya said, and swatted the air in his direction.

▍ Then, Out of Nowhere, It Just Comes to You

Francis stared at the grid and tried to think of a clue for a word that—he had no way of knowing—he would soon eject from the puzzle: "Homeless man's connection to loyal center."

I marveled how it tumbled out of his mind almost instantaneously.

"I do this for money, Dean."

The end of the clue is the cryptic part. *Connection* is a synonym for LINK. The "center" of the word *loyal* is OYA. The definition of *homeless man*, in this context, is LINKOYA.

▍ Nobody Does It for the Money

This is how much Francis and puzzle constructors like him earn for their efforts:

$300 for a cryptic crossword of this sort in the *New York Times*
$200 for a standard daily puzzle
$1,000 for a Sunday crossword
A labor of love defined.

Two Is Starting to Feel Like a Crowd

I ran into Bill Wasik on the street, blocks away from where I first met him a few years earlier when *The Next Big Thing* broke the story of flash mobs. We reported the first one, which Wasik instigated, at Claire's Accessories on Broadway.

I saw him on my way to the crossword tournament.

When I told him where I was headed, he replied, "Oh, Dean, I had no idea you were such a nerd!" He dragged out the last word in an especially mocking singsong: nerrrrrRRRRD!

The hierarchy of nerdhood came into sudden focus. It hadn't come as a surprise when my girlfriend at the time sent me off to the same tournament with: "Have fun with the nerds." (It was the last time I saw her, in fact.) Wasik, though, is different. He's an editor at *Harper's*. He even wears the trademark geek chic horn-rimmed glasses, for God's sake. And here he was calling *me* a nerd?

That gave me something to think about.

The Agony of Defeat

Now I understand why people watch sports.

It really had been a mystery to me until I took part in

the American Crossword Puzzle Tournament—the same year, coincidentally, documented in the film *Wordplay*.

Yes, it was exciting when twenty-year-old Tyler Hinman became the youngest champion in the history of the tournament. Hinman, then a student at Rensselaer Polytechnic Institute in Troy, New York, is eight years younger than the competition itself. Not only did he take the title from the reigning champ, Trip Payne of Boca Raton, Florida, but something else as well: until that day, Payne had been the youngest person (twenty-four years old) ever to win at Stamford.

But really, the competitor who made everyone's heart stop was Al Sanders. Sanders, once described by the *New Yorker* magazine as "a perennial also-ran from Colorado," breezed through the final-round puzzle at an astonishing speed, leaving Hinman and Payne in the dust. And while the Associated Press was accurate in reporting that Sanders "missed" the answer "Zolaesque," this did not take note of what had to have been the most heartbreaking moment in the history of this event: thinking he had finished the puzzle, Sanders did not look carefully enough at his grid and failed to notice that he had left two squares blank in the upper left-hand corner.

"Done!" he called out, and put his marker down. According to the rules of this contest, saying you are done cannot be undone.

"No!" shouted the crowd. "No!"

Sanders looked up and realized the catastrophe. Then he took the noise-blocking headphones that finalists wear and threw them to the floor. And then he sunk his face into his hands.

I've always assumed that when sports fans start shouting and throwing things, it's because they envision themselves on the court or the field. I have never in my life been an adequate enough athlete to imagine what it must be like to sink a three-pointer as the clock reaches zero or to hit a bases-loaded home run. Although my performance at the crossword tournament was merely fair, I could conceive of a day when—if I train for three hours per day during the next year—I might be better than average. But since I am a person who does crossword puzzles, I can at least fantasize about what it must be like up there on that stage.

That must explain the tears.

Nice Guys Really Do Finish Last (And That's Okay with Me)

According to one theory, the human attraction to puzzles is a remnant from the days when the very survival of our species depended on keen problem-solving abilities. That may be, but I'm beginning to have my doubts, especially after the large chunk of one hot summer day I spent participating in the Haystack, a nine-hour competitive puzzle that used the island of Manhattan as a playing board.

It was remarkable on several counts. The puzzles were very well made, and the organizers made ingenious use of the city, sending us from Marcus Garvey Park in Harlem to the Columbia campus, Times Square, Battery Park City, and finally Chinatown. Even more impressive, no one seems to have made any money from it. It was fun for its own sake—highly organized, extremely taxing fun for participants and organizers both. There was no admission fee, and the grand prize, the Golden Needle, was made from components procured at little cost from a hardware store.

My team—Unafraid, Laser-Honed Belfry Rejecter (I still have no idea how the name was derived, except that anagramming my name is what made us laser honed)—consisted of four veteran solvers for whom puzzles are a way of life. Plus me. We were by no means the only team approaching middle age, yet it seemed as if most of the players were, like the organizers, significantly younger (in their twenties and thirties), naturally fun loving, hip, and consistently attractive. On the surface it was a handful of teams competing against one another, but at a deeper level it was us versus the beautiful people.

Beautiful and crafty, I should add. Thanks to an element of the Haystack rules that was lost on our team, the key to winning ultimately had nothing to do with the ability to solve puzzles and everything to do with strategic thinking. The path to victory was reserved for those solvers who knew which puzzles not to bother with and, even more important, how to make use of Power Plays—sneaky tricks that, at their worst, could be used to force another team to swap its score with you.

Unafraid, Laser-Honed Belfry Rejecter made the fatal error of ignoring these Power Plays and instead plowed into the task of solving as many puzzles as we could. We got off to a terrific start, and after the organizers announced this fact to the other teams, one of them used the information to dump its low score on us and to steal our high point total. At that moment we went from second place to, I'm guessing, last. It knocked the wind out of our sails, about a third of the way through the game, and we never recovered. I took it in stride, which was rather uncharacteristic of me, but it set off one member of my team, who really let one of the organizers have it. (I wish to apologize now on that teammate's behalf.)

Then something happened that is very familiar to me. We grabbed the next round of puzzles and starting solving them with gusto, as if we knew there was no way we could compete in this arena—we're puzzlers, after all, not cutthroat competitors—so why not just enjoy ourselves? I could almost feel our collective blood pressure drop.

Is solving puzzles a vestige of a time when humans had to eat or be eaten? Given what happened at the Haystack, I'd be forced to argue just the opposite. It's what got us eaten. There are people who talk about puzzles as if they were a kind of competition with oneself. Perhaps, but that's not at all the same as competing against others. Puzzles and games get lumped together, but the two are opposites, really. If I ever again take part in one of these competitions, I'll propose to my teammates that we call ourselves the Ostriches and make a virtue of our tendency to plunge our heads into the sand, even as the Power Players make minced meat of us.

Inside the Puzzle Palace, or the Celebrification of Crosswords

The country's reigning crossword champion, twenty-year-old Tyler Hinman, sat in a breakfast nook in Utah struggling with the Saturday puzzle, the hardest of the week. The clock ticked on the *New York Times* crossword Web site—which meant his solving time would be posted for all the world to see—and most of the squares were blank.

He was nervous because his every move was being watched. The man looking over his shoulder was Will Shortz, who, along with Warren St. John, had just been recognized by readers of a gossip Web site (Gawker Hotties: Your Men of the 'Times') and who, for reasons not having to do with economic necessity, had the bottom bunk below Hinman, in a room they shared with Al Sanders and, in the trundle bed, me. They came to this condo in Deer Valley because, the next day, they would see themselves for the first time on the big screen at the world premiere of a documentary featuring them in starring roles, at the Sundance Film Festival.

In no way do I come close to Tyler's crossword-solving ability, and still I knew a little of what he was feeling. Earlier in the day I had pulled out my laptop as part of my morning routine. I looked around the table and realized I was surrounded by America's crossword royalty—Shortz, Hinman, Sanders, as well as former champion Ellen Ripstein—and I felt my testicles retract. I closed the computer and waited to have some time alone to finish the puzzle.

Hinman was unnerved, but what he could not see was that Shortz was smiling in awe at the speed with which he moved around the keyboard. Shortz teased him, saying that even to start the puzzle he'd have to resort to filling in the final *S*s of plurals. (Since clues and answers must agree in tense and number, it's usually easy to determine where to put a final *S*.) This seemed to be what was needed to jump-start things. The answers started to come. Hinman breezed through the rest of the puzzle and went on to finish in four minutes and sixteen seconds.

"Is everyone IMDb-ing themselves?" Ripstein asked as she passed through the kitchen.

"You bet," someone called out from another room inside the Puzzle Palace, which is what this condo was dubbed for the weekend. It was not a specific reference to James Bamford's book about the National Security Agency, titled *The Puzzle Palace*. Instead, it seems to have been the unconscious appropriation of a meme floating in the air, since, the previous month, it had been disclosed that the NSA had been secretly collecting data about telephone calls much more extensively than the public had realized. Perhaps the author's name had been forgotten or never known in the first place, but at one point, the title and the NSA were filed away for later use. This is an autonomic process among crossword solvers. Information soaks in as they pass through life, like plankton floating into the mouth of a whale.

Patrick Creadon, the director of *Wordplay*, announced to a crowd of moviegoers that the filmmakers wanted independence from Will Shortz, for the sake of credibility. Before long, however, Shortz's influence became evident. Thanks to a previous e-mail exchange with Shortz, I knew many of the celebrities on-screen were crossword solvers. When I first contacted him, I had a somewhat romantic notion that he might have ongoing correspondence with ordinary solvers from around the country. He responded that no, he didn't have time for that kind of thing, but he did provide me with this list of celebrity solvers (all were alive at the time):

A Few Famous People Who Solve Crosswords
by Will Shortz

1. Bill Clinton—When I interviewed him in 1992, he told me that he averages five to seven puzzles a week, and sometimes as many as three a day. He solved a puzzle of medium difficulty that I brought him in 6 minutes and 54 seconds, which was a good enough time to win a prize in a crossword tournament.
2. Beverly Sills
3. Bill Gates
4. Stephen King
5. Stephen Sondheim—who used to create cryptic crosswords for *New York* magazine
6. Richard Maltby Jr.—who still creates cryptic crosswords for *Harper's*
7. Ed Asner
8. Lee Iacocca
9. John Lithgow
10. Jane Curtin
11. Paul Sorvino
12. Teri Garr
13. Anne Meara
14. Dana Delany
15. Matthew Modine
16. Ellen Burstyn
17. Edie McClurg
18. Eli Wallach
19. Joan Rivers
20. Martha Stewart
21. Jon Stewart
22. Dick Gautier
23. Arte Johnson

24. Keith Hernandez
25. Tom Seaver
26. Yo-Yo Ma
27. Queen Elizabeth + much of the British royal family
28. Nora Ephron
29. Merv Griffin
30. Dick Cavett
31. Don Hewitt
32. Jill Sobule, singer
33. Ken Jennings, all-time greatest money-winner on *Jeopardy!*
34. Ken Burns—"Addiction: *New York Times* crossword puzzles. 'I do them every day,' says Burns. 'They give me infinite pleasure.'" (*USA Today*, 1/31/01)
35. Jack Kevorkian
36. Ira Levin—Solves the *New York Times* crossword every day (e-mails to WS, 2002)
37. Mike Mussina—"beloved *New York Times* crossword" (*Newsday*, 4/20/04)
38. Kate Hudson—"Instead of chilling out between scenes, Hudson feverishly completes crossword puzzles" (Louisville *Courier-Journal*, 5/28/04)
39. Bob Edwards—Solves the *New York Times*, *Washington Post*, and *USA Today* crosswords daily (*Milwaukee Journal Sentinel*, 4/25/04)
40. Greg Maddux
41. Lou Piniella
42. Bill Griffith, creator of the comic "Zippy"— "I do the *Times* puzzle every day—well, I skip Monday and Tuesday—too easy." (Letter to WS, 7/13/04)
43. Kim Komando, syndicated radio host—"I love crossword puzzles. Sundays are perfect for sitting

down with a cup of coffee, a crossword puzzle, and a lot of time." (www.komando.com, 9/12/04)

44. Lindsay Davenport—"Davenport waited out interminable rain delays—crossword puzzles were her salvation, she proclaimed." (*The Australian*, 9/10/04; plus other papers); "The Californian, who loves crossword puzzles and the simple, quiet life . . ." (*The Age*, Australia, 1/13/05)

45. Rose McGowan, actress on *Charmed*—According to Frank Longo, who met her at a karaoke bar, 12/14/04: "Said she does [crosswords] constantly, even in the bathtub, and has envisioned creating them. We spent a good fifteen minutes just talking about crosswordese and laughing about it." She mentioned Will Shortz before Frank did.

46. Brett Favre, Green Bay Packers quarterback—"Brett Favre . . . claims the only part of the [news]paper he uses is the crossword puzzle, and that's probably true." (*Wisconsin State Journal*, 12/26/04)

47. Kenneth Schermerhorn, director of the Nashville Symphony—"Favorite things to do . . . 2. Crossword puzzles. 'Either the Sunday *New York Times* crossword puzzle, or the Friday *Wall Street Journal* crossword.'" (Nashville *Tennessean*, 12/26/04)

48. Texas Rangers (various)—"Crossword puzzles and Frank Sinatra songs are morning staples in the Rangers' clubhouse before the workouts. . . . A number of Rangers are crossword buffs, including Conti, Kevin Mench, Greg Colbrunn, Rod Barajas, Doug Brocail and others. *USA Today* seems to be the favorite puzzle." (Fort Worth *Star-Telegram*, 3/3/05)

It's not surprising to me in and of itself that many of the Texas Rangers work on crosswords. It's obvious, when you think about it, that puzzles would make an appearance in any profession that involves lots of waiting around, be it in the dugout or the movie star's trailer or beside the radio host's microphone.

It is interesting when a powerful mind weighs in on the subject of crosswords. Joan Didion, in *The Year of Magical Thinking*, offers illuminating observations on how an empty grid can be a blank screen onto which we project the film of our grief after the sudden passing of a loved one:

> One morning during the spring after it happened I picked up *The New York Times* and skipped directly from the front page to the crossword puzzle, a way of starting the day that had become during those months a pattern, the way I had come to read, or more to the point not to read, the paper. I had never before had the patience to work crossword puzzles, but now imagined that the practice would encourage a return to constructive cognitive engagement. The clue that first got my attention that morning was 6 Down, "Sometimes you feel like . . ." I instantly saw the obvious answer, a good long one that would fill many spaces and prove my competency for the day: "a motherless child."
>
> *Motherless children have a real hard time—*
> *Motherless children have such a real hard time—*
> No.
> 6 Down had only four letters.
> I abandoned the puzzle (impatience died hard), and the next day looked up the answer. The

correct answer for 6 Down was "anut." "Anut?"
A nut? Sometimes you feel like a *nut*? How far
had I absented myself from the world of normal
response?

Notice: the answer most instantly accessed ("a
motherless child") was a wail of self-pity.

This was not going to be an easy failure of understanding to correct.

It's tempting to lament that our moment in history,
at the dawn of the twenty-first century, is more besotted
with celebrity than any other. In fact, our love affair with
fame goes way back. To capitalize on the tremendous success of their first publication, Simon & Schuster issued the
Celebrities' Cross Word Book, which featured puzzles said to
be constructed by famous people of the day. Will Shortz
said Margaret Farrar told him that all the "contributors"
tried to make a crossword, but only a couple actually made
legitimate puzzles, and that much of the book was written
by her and the other editors. This is how the celebrities
are identified in the table of contents.

"CONTRIBUTORS" TO *The Celebrities Cross Word Puzzle
Book* (SIMON & SCHUSTER, 1925)

1. Irving Berlin, composer
2. Alice Brady, actress
3. Heywood Broun, dramatic critic, columnist, author,
   and left end on the Harvard Cross Word Puzzle Team
4. Clare Briggs, cartoonist
5. Gelett Burgess, author of "The Goops"
6. Billie Burke, actress

7. Margaret Cameron, author
8. Eddie Cantor, actor
9. Feodor Chaliapin, opera singer
10. Marc Connelly, playwright and humorist
11. Frank Crowninshield, editor of Vanity Fair
12. Chauncey M. Depew, orator and publicist
13. John Farrar, editor of the Bookman
14. Morris Gest, theatrical producer
15. Alma Gluck, singer
16. Ruth Hale, critic, and president of the
    AMATEUR CROSS WORD PUZZLE
    LEAGUE OF AMERICA
17. Raymond Hitchcock, actor
18. Harry Houdini, magician
19. Owen Johnson, author
20. Al Jolson, actor
21. Newman Levy, writer
22. Cecilia Loftus, actress
23. Julian Mason, Managing Editor of the New York
    Herald Tribune
24. Neysa McMein, artist
25. Alice Duer Miller, author
26. Marilyn Miller, actress
27. Jay J. Morrow, Ex-Governor of the Panama Canal
    Zone
28. Pola Negri, motion picture star
29. Kathleen Norris, author
30. Neal O'Hara, writer
31. Anna Pavlowa, dancer
32. Ann Pennington, actress
33. Emily Price Post, author of "Etiquette"
34. Capt. Eddie Rickenbacker, Ace of Aces and motor
    magnate

35. Hugo Riesenfeld, motion picture impresario
36. Will Rogers, actor
37. Herb Roth, artist
38. S. D. Rothafel, ("Roxey"), movie impresario and radio star
39. Admiral William S. Sims, U. S. Navy
40. Governor Alfred E. Smith, Governor of New York
41. Dr. Sigmund Spaeth, music critic, author of "The Common Sense of Music," radio star and full back on the Princeton Cross Word Puzzle League
42. Herbert Bayard Swope, Executive Editor of the New York *World*
43. Deems Taylor, composer, and music critic of the New York *World*
44. William T. Tilden 2nd, tennis champion of the world
45. John Weaver and Peggy Wood, author and actress
46. H. T. Webster, cartoonist
47. Paul Whiteman, orchestra leader and emperor of jazz
48. Hendrik Willem van Loon, historian
49. Ruth Franc von Phul, Cross Word Puzzle Champion of the World
50. Efrem Zimbalist, violinist

The book's foreword refers to crosswords as the "literature of escape" and the "eighth lively art." I sigh.

History repeats itself in ways we can never anticipate. Just as crosswords and celebrities have a long history together, so, too, do crosswords and tournaments. Will Shortz believed he was creating something new when he founded the American Crossword Puzzle Tournament in 1978. His research into the history of his profession proved him wrong. In November of 1924, all comers were invited to compete in the auditorium at Wanamaker's department store, which seated one thousand. As the list above attests, the winner, Ruth von Phul, became an instant celebrity.

Several of the champion solvers featured in *Wordplay* reported that the highlight of their Sundance experience came when Glenn Close recognized them after a screening. I hold on to two special memories. The first is Trip Payne, bristling repeatedly at the term *word nerds* and regretting he ever said he was intrigued by the letter *Q*, the first line heard in the film. The second is Stamford Division B champion Amy Reynaldo, also known as Orange, at a reception hosted by the filmmakers, lamenting that her blog, Diary of a Crossword Fiend, required her to solve the *Times* puzzles Monday through Wednesday—something she never used to bother with because "I want to feel like a fucking genius when I'm done with a puzzle." A day without Orange is like a day without sunshine.

Nearly three years after its Sundance premiere, *Wordplay* is parodied by *The Simpsons*. The show has stayed on the air longer than anyone could have imagined. Crosswords aren't going anywhere soon. But the episode suggests that crossword celebrity itself has jumped the shark.

No Joy in Puzzleville

Socrates believed that education consists of extracting knowledge already inborn within all of us. This may be spiritual claptrap, but it's a comforting sentiment and it feels nice to say it. We get that same nice feeling whenever we are challenged by a difficult puzzle.

The *New York Times* crossword is one of the more difficult puzzles in American newspapers. It is also the most joyful. Those two things go together. The idioms, the wit, the broad cultural literacy required to solve it—all of these elements combine to create more than just an exhilarating Aha! experience (although, really, because of the satisfaction we derive from the makers' intelligence and creativity, we should call it the Ah! experience). It comforts us because it reminds us of things we already know, things deep inside us we feel we've known since before we were born.

There are, of course, lapses. I remember a Friday puzzle that was more difficult than usual. Under normal circumstances that would simply mean more time, greater focus, and, in the end, a more deeply satisfying experience. Something was different this time, though, and I wasn't the only one to notice. A lunch companion asked, "Hey Dean, what was wrong with today's puzzle?" The answer that jumped first to my lips: "It was joyless."

First, there was ETATIST. Who says that? The English word is "statist." Then came FOSDICK. Fosdick? And then LIBERTYPOLE. Huh? These are words that I and everyone I know would never, ever use. I wondered if they were provided by Crossword Compiler. It seemed as if the puzzle was obscure for the sake of difficulty, rather than difficult for the sake of satisfaction. The whole affair was less Aha! and more Wha?

I don't intend to disparage the constructor. After all, contributors to the *Times* online forum expressed how happy they were with the challenge. Was I turning into one of those people who want to reinforce who they have been rather than stretch into becoming someone new? That's the first sign of losing the battle of being alive. My hypothesis will be confirmed should I ever tune the radio to an oldies station.

Crossword as Narcosis

I wish I could have been there during the filming of *Annie Hall*, when Woody Allen gets irritated with the guy waiting in line behind him at the movies who is gassing off about the theories of media guru Marshall McLuhan. The guy declares himself an authority on the subject because he teaches a course at Columbia. Allen then fires back, "Really? Because I happen to have Mr. McLuhan right here!" McLuhan then shows up to tell the dopey professor he has no idea what he's talking about.

These kinds of misunderstandings were bound to happen with McLuhan, who tossed off gnomic assertions that sometimes seem dead-on and at other times dead wrong. If I were next in line, my question would have been: "Mr. McLuhan, did you *really* mean to write that radio is a hot medium? By your definition, it ought to be considered cold."

Next we'd discuss crosswords, particularly in light of his essay "The Gadget Lover: Narcissus as Narcosis." In it, McLuhan shows how we've gotten the myth all wrong. It's not that Narcissus loved himself; he thought his reflection was *someone else*.

McLuhan begins by pointing to the derivation of the hero's name. Put simply, Narcissus was numb. So numb he didn't even recognize his own image in the pond as himself.

It's an echo of the therapist who once asserted unequivocally that the characters in dreams are projections of the dreamer's self. Forget for a moment how much is unknown about why we dream. My thought was instead: How is this any different from our waking life?

McLuhan's love of jargon often turns his prose to sludge. It's easy to get sucked under by "extensions of the self" and "auto-amputation." In simpler terms, his point is that humans can flip out and be overwhelmed by intense emotion, so we cope by off-loading our selves into technology and media.

> We speak of "wanting to jump out of my skin" or of "going out of my mind," being "driven batty" or "flipping my lid." And we often create artificial situations that rival the irritations and stress of real life under controlled conditions of sport and play.

He then fails to list the supreme example of his point, which is the crossword puzzle. He didn't live to see the invention of the iTunes database, which demands that people like us correct inconsistent capitalization and alphabetize all artists and composers by last name. He never got to see the guy on the subway engrossed in Pong on his cell phone. People did not yet string the letters *OCD* together with the same ease they do now. But he understood all of these things.

For McLuhan, technology is an extension of the physical body—the central nervous system, in particular, the seat of our consciousness. I would add that, as with radio, the crossword is an extension of one's mental space. It is a validation of the contents of the self, mirrored back at us by the grid. We feel as if we're in communication with something outside ourselves, something that seems to know us, or speak directly to us, as it draws out information we've been storing inside.

Some Orthodox Jews extend the idea of the household by stretching a string, called an *eruv*, around their neighborhood, so that any activity allowed only in the home on the Sabbath is therefore extended to the space defined by the *eruv*. I think of the crossword as a mental *eruv*.

McLuhan has sobering things to say about *why* we relate to technology and media as we do. It's how we manage trauma. We're in shock.

By extension, we have something to learn by considering how trauma and shock may push us toward crosswords. This is how denial works. Being aware of it in your head does nothing to protect you from it. The coping strategies that keep us alive as children end up killing us as adults. As self-deceptions go, it's an elaborate one but necessary, as it makes everyday life possible. *Quod me nutrit me destruit.*

With no knowledge of any of this, my father used me to create a visual representation of McLuhan's theories. It happened when I was in my early teens and playing a lot of musical instruments. Perhaps it is more accurate to say that I played "at" them. Dad, in his charitable moments, called me a Renaissance man, and at other times a jack of all trades, master of none. He once photographed me wearing a band outfit suitable for the time—a white turtleneck and burgundy blazer—playing each of the instruments in my arsenal. Then he cut away everything outside my silhouette and made a diorama: an orchestra of me, playing with myself.

Thanks to modern electronics, it is now easier than ever

for a musician to realize McLuhan's echo chamber, and indeed loopers and laptops have allowed the comeback of the one-man band. Some voice of sanity deep within has warned me not to head down that road.

Seven Types of Ambiguity (More, Actually)

"Where's my—? Somewhere I have a list of cryptic indicators. Scooch over."

Francis was talking to me but could just as easily have been addressing one of the cats, which had been hanging out with us awhile and needed to be evicted.

He apologized to the cat for taking away the pile of clothes she slept on, and continued: "She's a sort of unsatisfactory cat for lap sitting because she doesn't like to sit still. She's just neurotic. Her mother knew how to sit. But she got ill and she is dead." Francis continued, *sotto voce*, "I liked her mother better." And then, to the cat: "Good thing you don't know English because you'd be more fucked up than you are."

Francis considered putting the cats into the puzzle he was constructing, in a roundabout way. SENILE might have been nice, since it is "felines" backward, minus the F. Ultimately, though, it couldn't make its way into the grid.

Deep in a pile, he found what he had been looking for: a printout he had bought years earlier for $15 from another constructor at a puzzle convention.

"My filing system comes through!"

The sheaf of pages contained lists of words that can be used in the service of making cryptic clues. Compared to his electronic arsenal, which includes a Web site that finds phrases in Wikipedia, the printout seemed quaint.

Really, the opportunities for wordplay have not changed all that much since cryptic crosswords first started appearing in the 1920s. In *Ximenes on the Art of the Crossword*, D. S. Macnutt catalogues seven main types and then provides an addendum of other options that appear less frequently.

I hesitate before listing them here because this is usually the freak-out moment for people I try to initiate into the ways of cryptic crosswords. Their feelings of inadequacy are so strong I can smell them. So let's make a deal. I'll go through the options here, and if you feel your throat starting to close, just skip over them and remind yourself that the key is to think hyperliterally.

First, though, I'd like to emphasize that Macnutt, aka Ximenes, believed that first and foremost his job as a clue writer was to be *fair* to the solver. Several times he repeats a mantra from a predecessor, A. F. Ritchie ("Afrit"), who made puzzles for the *Listener* magazine: "I need not mean what I say, but I must say what I mean."

I have encountered this sentence on multiple occasions and I confess it fails to crystallize the point in my mind as intended. I was relieved to learn that Ximenes himself struggled with its meaning, saying it "in itself is a little cryptic to the uninitiated; I'm inclined to put it the wrong way round myself when I don't think!"

Here's a clear and literal translation of Afrit's maxim: the clue intends to deceive you, but it *must* indicate, completely and fairly, how to decipher it.

This concern regarding fairness is a reaction to an anything-goes cryptic tradition that started with Torquemada and continues among some present-day setters. Don Manley calls these non-Ximenean clues "wild and woolly" and worries they're far too common. I raised a famous one with him: HIJKLMNO. The answer is WATER. The cryptic indicator is there—*H* "to" *O*—but the definition is missing.

Manley acknowledged that including the definition would make it less elegant, but he disapproves of anything that deteriorates the soundness of a clue. "The secret is to obey the rules and to get it elegant as well."

Here, then, are a few of the primary forms of wordplay as outlined by Ximenes. I've decided against reprinting his examples, however. They're very British and, I fear, a deterrent, given our purposes here. One note: according to the conventions of cryptic crosswords, the length of the word or words in the answer is indicated in parentheses. If you see *(7)*, that means the answer consists of a single seven-letter word; *(3,4)* tells you to come up with a three-letter word followed by a four-letter word.

1. Two or more meanings. American constructors tend to call these double definitions. The *Guardian* offers this example: "Savings book (7) = RESERVE. Your savings are a reserve and you can book/reserve, say, a ticket."

2. Reversals. The *New Yorker* magazine gave this example of a reversal for newcomers to its cryptic crossword, which ran during the Tina Brown era in the very late 1990s: "Returned beer of kings (5). A word meaning *beer*, written backward, will yield the answer, a word meaning *of kings*: REGAL. In some clues, known as down clues, the indicator may suggest that a word be written upward.

For example, the answer to 'Ambush split up (4)' is TRAP (ambush), which is PART (split) written upward. In reversal clues the indicator is always beside the definition of the word being reversed, not the definition of the answer. Words or phrases like *backward, in retreat, heading west,* or, in down clues, *rising* and *northward,* may signal a reversal."

3. Charades. Who hasn't noticed that THERAPIST is made up of two shorter words? Here's an example from the *Atlantic* Puzzler's instructions: "A clue may break the answer into two or more convenient parts and define them sequentially, as in the game of charades. FARMING (agriculture) breaks into 'far' (remote) and 'Ming' (Chinese dynasty), and could be clued as 'Agriculture in remote Chinese dynasty (7).'"

That's enough for the moment. We can go through other cryptic clue types after a breather.

Reading Ximenes, there are several things to like about him. For one, he calls people who make puzzles "composers," which has a nice ring to it and fits with my own abandoned aspirations. He shares my distaste for *paronomasia,* which "can become monotonous, as puns in conversation undoubtedly can, and must not be overdone." (I like the fancy term that Ximenes used because it sounds like a mental disorder.) And he expresses exasperation with crossword practice in the United States: "Though the crossword puzzle there is over fifty years old, definition clues are still the normal thing. There must be, however, voices there crying in the wilderness."

There are. Allow me to introduce myself. I'm John the Baptist.

I found a kindred spirit in Stephen Sondheim. At least I thought I did when I read an essay by him on the superiority of cryptic crosswords. It appeared as the foreword to a collection of puzzles he created for *New York* magazine during its earliest days and was adapted from an article he wrote in 1968 to introduce readers of the debut issue to this alien puzzle style. He begins with an especially worthy manifesto.

> The kind of crossword puzzle familiar to most Americans is a mechanical test of tirelessly esoteric knowledge: "Brazilian potter's wheel," "East Indian betel nut" and the like are typical definitions, sending you either to *Webster's New International* or to sleep. The other kind, prevalent in Great Britain but until recently non-existent in the United States apart from *The Nation*, *The Atlantic*, and *Harper's*, is a test of wits. This kind of puzzle offers cryptic clues instead of bald definitions, and the pleasures involved in solving it are the deeply satisfactory ones of following and matching a devious mind (that of the puzzle's author) rather than the transitory ones of an encyclopedic memory.
>
> To call the composer of a crossword an author may seem to be dignifying a gnat, but clues in a "cryptic" crossword have many of the characteristics of a literary manner: cleverness, humor, even a pseudo-aphoristic grace. In the best puzzles, styles of clue-writing are distinctive, revealing special pockets of interest and small mannerisms, as in

any prose style. The clues of the author who called himself "Ximenes" in the London *Sunday Observer* were, to the eye of a puzzle fan, as different from those in, say, the Manchester *Guardian* as Wilde is from Maugham. But a "Bantu hartebeest" remains a "Bantu hartebeest" whether it's in *The New York Times* or the *Daily News*.

Railway coaches, undergrounds, lunch counters and offices in England hum with the self-satisfied chuckles of solvers who suddenly get the point of a clue after having stared at it for several baffled minutes. Bafflement, not information, is the keystone of a cryptic puzzle. A good clue can give you all the pleasures of being duped that a mystery story can. It has surface innocence, surprise, the revelation of a concealed meaning, and the catharsis of solution. Solving a British puzzle is far more rewarding than dredging up arcane trivia, and it is not annoyingly difficult once you've been initiated into the methods of solution. It's a matter of mental exercise, not academic clerk work, and all it takes is inexhaustible patience, limitless time and an eccentric mind.

It was gratifying to learn that Sondheim saw a literary aspect in British-style puzzles, but the word that clinched it—my certainty that he was a fellow traveler—was *catharsis*, which Aristotle defined, in his *Poetics*, as the purgation of strong emotions such as pity and fear.

There was yet more shock of recognition reading Meryle Secrest's biography of Sondheim.

Sondheim said he had only recently realized that his interest in games and conundrums dated from the failure of his parents' marriage, and that moment when "nothing made sense any more [sic]." The puzzle was a metaphor, a reassurance he desperately needed that there really was a path through the maze, that magical secrets waited to be revealed, that a world in fragments could be reassembled, however painfully, and that a key existed to every riddle if he searched diligently enough. For that reason he was never interested in games in which the rules were flexible and open to challenge. These did not suit him at all. He wanted games for which the rules were inflexible, where one always knew exactly what was coming next, as in military school, as if to "face out the black terrors of life," as Anthony Shaffer wrote in *Sleuth*.

I wrote to Sondheim, inviting him to discuss this idea further, inserting into the letter my aforementioned belief that pitting emotions against ideas is a false dichotomy. This was itself meant as a cryptic clue, a hint that I did not subscribe to the perception that his musicals are intellectual at the expense of feeling. Sondheim wrote back that he was not particularly interested in the "emotional essence" of crosswords, but that he would be happy to tell me about his role in introducing cryptic puzzles to the United States.

His house is, as advertised, decorated with games and puzzles, a motif Shaffer borrowed when writing *Sleuth*— the playwright based the Laurence Olivier role on him— and a reminder that one working title of the play was *Who's Afraid of Stephen Sondheim?*

Our conversation consisted of a series of attempts by me to extract concessions from him and to reconcile his words on the page with the words he uttered on the couch, while he repeatedly scratched his beard and looked off to the left and almost never directly in the eye.

Had he noticed what seemed to be a high concentration of cryptic puzzle makers in the world of musical theater?

He hadn't.

"Oh, I don't think it's any different than making puzzles and making any kind of art. I mean, you know, it's about design. It's not just musical theater. It's not just music, either."

It occurred to me that perhaps there only seemed to be a high percentage simply because there were so few cryptic puzzles in America in the first place, and this paucity of puzzles has given undue prominence to Sondheim and his successor at *New York*, the Broadway lyricist Richard Maltby, who continues to make the monthly cryptic crossword for *Harper's* magazine. Then there was the story Sondheim had told the British music writer Norman Lebrecht about how the toughest crossword puzzle in England, published weekly by the BBC magazine, figured in his own early days in the theater: "The *Listener* was published Wednesday and would reach the U.S. on Thursday. I'd grab a copy on my way to work on *West Side Story*, and I got Leonard Bernstein hooked. Thursday afternoons no work got done on *West Side Story*. We were doing the puzzle."

Sondheim said to me: "There *is* a correlation between music and medicine and math—the Three *M*s. There is a mathematical aspect to puzzle making which has to do with a kind of geometry of language and the ability to dissect words as collections of letters rather than as vehicles of meaning. Just the way making music is assembling a group of artificial sounds—notes—into something that one could term a composition. And in that sense, a cross-word puzzle is a composition. It has a form, a shape, a recognizable style, even."

I continued with what seemed to be a no-brainer—the close kinship between fitting words into a grid and fitting lyrics into a melody. Sondheim equivocated.

"Yeah, I suppose so. But also deciding on the color of the tree is the same kind of—you know," he said. "All art, in that sense, is a kind of puzzle, so it's a *reductio ad absurdum*, I think. Any kind of choice is a puzzle, if you want to use the world *puzzle*. No, I think, there's a certain analogy in my head between lyric writing and puzzle making in the sense that you're dealing with a problem for which there is a limited number of solutions. Again, the problem is, there may be no solution, whereas with a crossword puzzle, there always is. Although you know about Max Beerbohm's famous puzzle."

He was referring to a perverse and maddening stunt pulled by the English writer and caricaturist who, in the March 9, 1940, issue of the *Times* of London, published a crossword that had no answer—an itch that could never be scratched.

I then pushed Sondheim toward the aspect of his essay that had interested me the most—the idea that cryptic puzzles are in some way akin to literature. Both, after all, are about creating an experience for the end user, about delineating a mental space.

"No, I really think of it as a pastime. Perhaps every pastime is a way of creating a space for yourself. So, you know, needlepoint: Is there any difference?"

It was clear he thought I was giving puzzles more credit than they deserved. And yet, I reminded him, he was the one who made the connection to Aristotle in the first place.

"I doubt if I said it was all about catharsis. If I did, then I was exaggerating."

We chatted about other things—about the highly regarded revival of *Sunday in the Park with George* running at the time in a renovated chocolate factory in London, and about the *New York Times* puzzle and how Will Shortz has done wonders for it.

Before I left, I gave it one more try. I mentioned his tumultuous relations with his family, including one parent so narcissistic that Sondheim once wrote to a friend, "Thanks for the plate, but where was my mother's head?" I told him about the impact of my own parents' divorce on me and how it rang true when I read, in the Secrest biography, that he traced a line from the breakup of his mother and father to his involvement with puzzles.

"Did I talk about puzzles in relation to my mother? No kidding."

I read the passage back to him.

"Yeah, it's order out of chaos." He said it very fast, repeatedly, and faster each time—orderoutofchaos—to the point that it became an empty signifier, stripped completely of the anguish it was intended to represent.

"Sure, orderoutofchaos. But again, it's a *reductio ad absurdum*, because as far as I'm concerned, that's what art is. It's making orderoutofchaos, whether it's sound, meaning music, or whether it's visual. It's orderoutofchaos. It's what artists do. That's the definition of the profession."

It was a reluctant concession, but there it was. He equated crosswords with art. And then he issued this qualification: "Constructing a puzzle, and even solving one but particularly constructing one, is a minor form of a minor art. And as such, you are making and you are communicating. And that's what it's all about."

I ended up seeing the London production of *Sunday in the Park with George* and decided it was unfair to expect Sondheim to say in an interview what he showed so perfectly on the stage.

Banner Hanging from the High Line in Chelsea

> An artist who speaks about his art for more than one
> minute is lying.
>
> —Patrick Mimran

No One Ever Became a Hit at Parties by Excelling at Crossword Puzzles

One evening at a dinner I sat next to Sara Fishko, a respected colleague from WNYC who also plays the piano. I mentioned I was considering taking lessons again, something I had abandoned in college. What drew me to the idea was a book I had just read by a teacher for whom practicing the piano was a spiritual discipline, an exercise in mindfulness. I thought it would be a worthwhile way to work through some things.

"Why don't you just go into analysis?" she asked in her trademark deadpan that carried with it the implied epithet "you dumbass."

Yes, but. There is so much bad therapy in the world, and I've spent so much money on it. This way I stood a chance of at least becoming a better pianist.

You Would Be Surprised How Handy It Is to Be a Crossword Puzzle Person at Parties

"People are fascinated," Francis said, twisting his head toward me and taking a much-needed break from the computer screen. "The conversation is dead, and I mention that I write puzzles, and I've got a good five minutes to go on 'How do you do that?'"

This gave me more incentive to take up puzzle construction. Usually, my cocktail-party chat goes like this:

I mention that the *New York Times* publishes its most difficult puzzle on Saturdays.

"Really?" the other person will say. "I thought it was Sundays."

"No, Sunday is the largest crossword of the week, but it's usually pitched at a difficulty level of a Wednesday or Thursday puzzle."

Silence.

Three Places in New Jersey

Garden State Parkway, near Perth Amboy

I have little recollection of life before the age of sixteen, the year I left for college. I do remember being driven by my father to the Food & Fuel near where the Parkway intersects with the New Jersey Turnpike. It was the midpoint between the house where I grew up, not far from Clinton, New Jersey, and the series of places my mother moved to on the Jersey Shore after I was eight. On Fridays he would take me there. Not bring me there, take me—a recurring mistake of mine he often corrected. My mother would have me for the weekend, and then on Sundays the routine was repeated in reverse. Dad broke the silences by playing a game he called Trivia, in which he asked me questions and I answered them. I have never seen a Tarzan movie, but I will always remember that the apeman was played by multiple actors, including the Olympic swimming champion Johnny Weissmuller.

The Apartment of My Stepfather's Parents, in Long Branch

I am nine and a half years old. My mother and stepfather have accused me of some sort of wrongdoing. I have mounted a defense that involves pacing back and forth across the living room. They find this funny and tell me to stop being a lawyer. As a result I seriously begin to consider a career in the legal profession.

A Garden Apartment in Secaucus, Five Years Later

Actually, behind the apartment, in an empty lot strewn with trash. It is a matter of weeks before my mother will pack a bag and walk me past my stepfather, who is yelling loudly as she takes me to the car and drives us to safety at the Holiday Inn on Route 9. It will be at least five more years before the two of them start preceding "alcoholic" with "recovering." On this night, though, before those other developments have occurred, I am grunting from deep within my chest as I take a piece of driftwood and beat it against a rock.

There. Who needs to spend money on a therapist to understand why it's so important for me to be right?

Of course, as anyone who has been beaten up in the schoolyard can tell you, needing to be right all the time is maladaptive. Plus, I think it is the reason why I find humor about stupid people to be unfunny. I do make an exception for *The Big Lebowski*. It is endlessly hilarious to hear John Goodman say, "Shut the fuck up, Donny."

One Down

I was flat on my back on the patio. Somehow—I don't know how it happened—I had suffered a serious laceration to the neck. My fiancée stood in the doorway as I, unable to speak, reached to my throat to show her just how urgently I needed her. I touched the severed end of an artery, wide as a rubber feeding tube but much more elastic and collapsed because there was no blood left to maintain its shape. It was then I could feel that the cut had gone clean through and my head was separated from my body.

Twenty-five years later, it seems obvious that this dream served as a caution against the dangers of living, as we say these days, too much in one's own head. Still, I've spent my life ignoring its warning, most flagrantly when it comes to my crossword puzzle habit.

To Dream the Impossible Dream

Horses were lying on the living room floor. Under normal circumstances, they should have been able to speak to me, but these horses were sick—so sick they could only look up at me with pained expressions.

The dream was still vivid in my mind when I opened the door for Alfred, who was scheduled to tune my piano first thing in the morning. My defenses down, I told him all the details.

"Oh, it's a very Swiftian dream."

I was too groggy to grasp his meaning.

"You know, the Houyhnhnms."

I told him it seemed like a stretch, since I hadn't read *Gulliver's Travels* in years and it was unlikely they'd be on my mind.

Without prompting, Alfred went on to interpret the dream. "The horses are your animal side. Your feelings. You're not in touch with them." And then he tuned the piano.

How Alfred nailed it, in a matter of seconds, is beyond me. I suppose it's possible I might have arrived at this interpretation on my own, after a pot of coffee. I can say with confidence that I've never had a therapist as perceptive as Alfred, who started referring to himself as my Jungian piano tuner.

■ On Solving the Crossword with Someone Else

I don't think of myself as tentative, but my crossword-solving habits have led at least one cosolver to apply that description to me. It's true that using a pen makes me more careful. That's because a cleanly filled grid with no cross-outs is infinitely more satisfying than a quickly filled grid. Pencils, and the inevitable erasures that go along with them, bring ugliness into the universe.

If I had to divide people into two types, I would do it this way: those who solve crosswords in pencil and those who use a pen. I suppose pencil and pen people could be allowed to work on puzzles together; however, that way madness lies. Pencil people, even when they use pens out of courtesy, approach the puzzle with—dare I say it?—a certain recklessness. They've developed this habit because they think everything can be erased. Yes, pencils have erasers, but the mind does not.

Take, for example, a puzzle that ran in the Saturday *Times*. Once RANTER was there ("One given to diatribes"), it was hard to see the grid with fresh eyes so that SPEWER could take its place. And it was all I could do to keep from blurting out, "No! Don't put in ANTHER!! Sure, it may be an 'Iris part,' but chances are they're not talking about flowers, they mean the one in your eye!!!" Crossword etiquette demands keeping such impulses in check.

Or does it? There are plenty of people in this world who solve puzzles happily as a team. I have never been among them. No matter how I try to modulate my behavior, something I do intimidates solving partners, tamping down the confidence of friends who otherwise manage just fine on their own. As a result, I mostly observe a self-imposed crossword solitude.

That particular Saturday, however, was an exception. Eventually, we changed the answer to AREOLE. Those potentially right but ultimately wrong answers seared themselves into our brains, keeping the northeast and southwest quadrants empty for a couple of hours, until finally we rebuilt from scratch.

Don't get me wrong. I'm the first to admit that my love of a neat, ink-filled grid is as OCD as my iTunes library. I do think, though, that there is an argument to be made for keeping your options open by leaving squares blank—the mind a *tabula rasa*—until certainty is achieved. It's more efficient in the long run. I realize, too, that this line of reasoning is headed in a direction that will seem to contradict my previous statements about racing against the clock. Really, though, my complaint has less to do with speed solving and more to do with avoiding the wrong path, which equals unnecessarily lost time. If time does indeed equal money, then pen people rule.

I'll Crush You with My Pencil, Dude

"Don't go pen versus pencil with me," Francis said. "I'll smash you like a bug."

Understood. Perhaps, then, we should consider what other types of cryptic clues Francis had at his disposal in making his puzzle.

4. Container and contents. From the *Mensa Cryptic Crosswords* books: "If the answer breaks into convenient parts not side by side but one within the other, the clue may say that one part 'contains,' 'holds,' 'grips,' or even 'swallows' the other. CALLOW (inexperienced, green) has 'all' inside 'cow,' yielding the clue: Bovine has eaten everything green (6)." Here's another example from Cox and Rathvon—an unintentional tip of the hat to Sir Jeremy: "Sullen operator entering code (6)." When *operator*, or O, is "entering" Morse *(code)*, you get MOROSE, which is a synonym for *sullen*.

5. Puns. That's what Ximenes called them. I prefer to call them homophones, which is not an exact synonym. The difference is, in my view,

that the former is a type of humor based on the latter. And I have to confess my view that there is no difference between a good pun and a bad pun. Stephen Sondheim, in the introduction to his collected puzzles, presents a particularly apt (for him) example: "Some clues deal with homonyms—words of different meaning which have the same sound. Indications of them usually consist of phrases like 'we hear' and 'sounds like,' as in *We hear the musical is German* (4). The musical is *'Hair'* and we hear it as HERR (German as a single noun)."

The Weaver's Tale

I arrived at the weaver's house at six in the morning. There was no risk of waking him.

"Thank God the paper is arriving as early as four thirty, which is perfect for me," he said.

I had come to watch a remarkable ritual he observed each morning. He woke up before the dawn and filled in the crossword lightly, in pencil. Then he erased it, leaving a blank grid for his wife.

The reason, he said, was that his wife is smart, and he a self-avowed moron. Working on the puzzle together was not an option because she was so fast at it.

"There's no way I can even think about the *New York Times* crossword. Even for this dopey *Eagle* puzzle, which a chimpanzee could do with its eyes closed, I have a hard time." The *Berkshire Eagle* prints a crossword syndicated by the *Chicago Tribune* that is not known for its quality.

The weaver then produced equipment necessary

for the morning's task. "I'm very happy to say that I've acquired some carpentry pencils with proper erasers. This is for the final erasure, after I've either finished or had no success with the puzzle, and I'm ready to leave for work."

I had heard him mention the ritual at a dinner party. On that occasion, he performed his story with a mock outrage that is at the center of his humor. This morning he explained his position with a much more measured tone.

"I believe that the protocol is: it's an obligation to read the paper—all sections—and then finally end up at the puzzle. Sometimes she'll just go right at the puzzle."

He then dropped his pitch and volume together.

"I don't think that's right. Do you?"

These self-imposed rules have caused difficulty for the weaver, especially on days when he has woken up late.

"If I'm just getting into the paper, and I hear her scampering about upstairs, the moment she comes through that door, I will pretend I've gone through the paper first."

By that, he meant he would take the various sections and put them in disarray.

"And then I'll be on the Berkshire section. I'll be pretending to read that, and then just casually move on, to what I'm really interested in."

His rules stipulated that what happened next would secure his rights.

"Once you have the crossword open, it's yours."

In the weaver's view of things, his system worked only if he got to the puzzle first.

"Here's the problem: she presses down so hard with

her pencil that when she erases it, it's like doing a grave marking. It's still there, no matter what. Even if she completely erases, she'll have that indentation. Whereas when I do it, I barely put it in, so it's easy to erase."

He sighed deeply.

"Now, see, this is going to be sad today, because I don't think I'm going to be able to get any of these. 'Literally, bait.' What the hell does that mean? Aw, jeez."

"My feeling is if you only get less than half of the puzzle done, you don't erase it. It's a fifty-fifty deal. You do half, she does half." It sounded like the perfect marriage.

He offered no reply.

Were there ever times they worked on the puzzle together?

Yes, said the weaver. Especially difficult ones. They usually did the Sunday crossword together. But never the *Times*.

"No, it would just make me feel bad. Why would I want to do that? It's stupid. You know? *That's* stupid. To literally get up first thing in the morning and do something that makes you feel like an idiot? I don't think so.

"Oh, this is sad. Why couldn't we have done this little gathering on a Monday?"

It was only partly the weaver's fault. This puzzle had some especially bad flaws. First, there was the inconsistency of the theme clues. If this were a *Times* puzzle, they would all conform to the same style. These did not. Then there was the answer PSU. Pennsylvania State University is shortened to Penn State. Never PSU.

"Evil," said the weaver. "Cruel. Nasty."

It wasn't really any of those things. Just poorly made.

The weaver's wife was still in bed when he finished the crossword. I drove to a coffee shop to wait until she woke up. By the time I got back she was done with the puzzle.

Six months later, their marriage had ended.

Meetings with Remarkable Men, Part 2: Order Amid Chaos

SCENE—New York's Upper East Side, the home office of Richard Maltby, lyricist, director, producer and screenwriter, who succeeded Stephen Sondheim as the creator of the *New York* magazine puzzle. Sondheim left the job when he went off to write *Company*, the Broadway musical that made him into the most important creator of musical theater in our time. Maltby took the job until it was time for him to conceive *Ain't Misbehavin'*—one of the first jukebox musicals—which won him a Tony award for Best Director. Maltby is now the sole creator of variety cryptics for *Harper's*.

[Son enters.]

SON. Hey Dad, old buddy.

MALTBY [*to son*]. Are you short of money? Speak to your friend here.

MALTBY [*to me*]. It always costs twenty dollars to get an expression of love from your child, which I consider to be a reasonable price.

It is the most unobtrusive interruption of the interview, conducted soon after the opening of a troubled show on Broadway. Remarkably, the numerous phone calls fail to derail his train of thought.

MALTBY. Right now, I just had a show opening. Was I going to get a puzzle in? No. Actually, for the first time, I said, "Let's reprint a puzzle from the past. I can't do one this time."

Unlike Sondheim, Maltby agrees that there does seem to be a greater than usual amount of interest in puzzles among musical theater people, citing lyricist Sheldon Harnick (Fiddler on the Roof) *and the composer/lyricist Stephen Schwartz* (Godspell, Pippin, Wicked).

MALTBY. There's a reason for that. If you write lyrics, you deal with words and language on a technical level that no one else deals with. I happen to write to music. I like it when David writes the music first.

The composer David Shire is Maltby's frequent collaborator.

MALTBY. So you can imagine what I'm really writing is: a sentence that is this long, has this many syllables, has the accents here, here, and here, and says what I wanted to say, which preexists the setting of the line—
[He leaves the room to take a call. He comes back and picks up the thought exactly where he left it.]
MALTBY.—so you're dealing with language completely technically. And the other thing that you really understand in lyric writing: it exists in time and comes at you. And that's where the vagaries of the English language can come back and bite you in the nose. You can write a sentence, and then it's

sung, and then it turns out that same phrase has another meaning.

OLSHER. "And we like sheep."

It's a line from Isaiah—"And we, like sheep, have gone astray"—that undergoes an unintentionally hilarious transformation in Handel's Messiah *when the chorus repeats the first four words to a rhythm that obliterates those essential commas and makes it sound as if they sing in praise of tasty mutton.*

MALTBY. "And we like sheep!" Exactly. I did this ridiculous musical called *Nick and Nora*, which had a line in it—Arthur Laurents wrote it—and no one ever noticed it until we said it out loud in front of an audience. It was about a woman who had quit a job on the East Coast and came to California, and the guy who was telling the story said, "And she took a little dump up in the hills." Nobody caught it until you heard it out loud.

[The phone rings.]

MALTBY. And I have a theory about that, and this is why I think these kinds of puzzles exist only in the English language—because the language is so complex.

[Phone rings.]

MALTBY. Hold the thought.

[Takes another phone call. Returns.]

MALTBY. The theory is, there is no such thing as the English language. The English language is an entirely borrowed language. You know, there's Anglo-Saxon for all the basic words like *cow* and *house*, and then there's the French invasion, which brought in *beef* and *veal* and *mansion* and all the upper-class words, and then it was Catholic, all the Latinisms come in, laid over. And then the Empire: Muslim words, Indian words. And so the language is piled high with borrowed things, and as a result, meanings have shifted and a word can take on a dozen meanings. It's only really true—I don't know about other languages, but certainly in the Romance languages, in French and Italian, words mean pretty much what they mean. But English, everything sort of means different things, and as a result, by creating a sentence, which is a context, you can mislead, you can suggest that you mean this when in fact you mean that.

It's such an attractive idea. Colin Dexter made a similar claim, that no other language could have given birth to cryptic crosswords, a belief he attributes to the preponderance of homonyms. It makes me wonder if my mother was onto something when she exclaimed, "What an amazing language!" Is it the most amazing language of all? Later I will run this by Will Shortz, who disagrees completely. He draws my attention to the enormous popularity of crosswords in Italy, home to a weekly puzzle publication, La settimana enigmistica, *since 1932. This prompts me to contact Marcel Danesi, an Italian-born scholar of puzzles in Toronto who seems insulted by the ridiculousness of the notion that English is somehow uniquely suited to ambiguity: "If you don't believe me, just read Dante!" I forgive Maltby because he appears, at first, anyway, to agree with me that our advertising culture should already have primed America for cryptic crosswords.*

MALTBY. People think that Americans don't like to use the complexity of language, but look at any of the famous slogans. It's all about puns. Every single one of those slogans is a sentence with at least two meanings.

[CUT TO—a bus ad from designer Kenneth Cole: WE'RE ALL FORGETTING AIDS. FOR and GETTING are printed in different colors, forcing the viewer to consider the double meaning: "We're dismissing the AIDS crisis/We're in favor of contracting AIDS."]

I cling to my fantasy of bringing cryptics to widespread popularity in the United States. Any hope that I will be able to conscript Maltby to join my crusade is soon dashed when he goes on to imply he does not think cryptic crosswords will take the country by storm anytime soon.

MALTBY. I think they're a little abstruse. People think Americans are too literal-minded, where, in fact, I point to ads to say we are not. We understand the multiplicity of the language automatically. But that's not to say we love to wallow in it. It takes a particular kind of demented mind.

I decide not to tell Maltby that when I was a child my favorite musical was Man of La Mancha. *My aesthetic tastes have grown since then, but I still consider Quixote's idealism a suitable and appropriate template for how to live one's life. The phone rings again. This time, Maltby stays in the room while he takes the call, which lasts seventeen minutes and fifty seconds. It is from an actor in the show that has just opened, who shouts so loudly I can hear everything he says, except for the moments when his volume is so overwhelming, the sound is distorted. Among the sentences he screams at Maltby: "Does anyone fucking give a shit anymore!" "I haven't seen any of you mother-*

fuckers!" "I just want someone to fucking listen to me!" "I don't believe you guys as far as I can fucking throw you, and that's not far!" "You guys are a bunch of fucking pussies!" "I haven't seen any of you jackasses in a fucking month and a half!" Maltby tries to answer calmly but his tone follows the singsong pitch patterns of a parent losing his patience. The end of the call is followed by a pause.

MALTBY. He's not—worth it. If I had any sense I would have fired him a long time ago.

The call most definitely changes the tenor of our dialogue. Maltby rebounds quickly, however. Before long the conversation turns to "Crossword Puzzle," a song he wrote with David Shire that appeared in their musical revue Starting Here, Starting Now. *It's sung by a know-it-all woman who, while working on the* New York Times *crossword, finally comes to an understanding of why her man has left her.*

MALTBY. In her case, it was being too smug, being too smart-ass, too smug about her own intelligence that drove him away.
OLSHER. For me, anyway, I've found that it's impossible to find togetherness over a puzzle because I have the same qualities she has and it's all I can do to—
MALTBY. Oh, to stop being smug? She couldn't stop being either smug, because she knew the answer, or patronizing: "Oh, I won't give you the answer, I'll let you find the answer." "I'll let him hold the pencil." "I'll come up with the answers but he'll write the words in." She just had no idea until the last line of the song it was *that* that drove him

away. He simply couldn't stand how patronizing she was. People have sort of parsed that. There's an awful lot of character in that. She's the one with the doctorate. She's the one who had all the education, she's the one who just wanted everybody to know how smart she was. At that time—actually, the song is a little dated because Will Shortz wouldn't allow those words in anymore. He banned "crossword puzzle" words from the puzzles.

I consider taking issue with this. While it is true that Shortz has made great headway in this regard, still I grimace whenever a puzzle calls for the ARAL Sea or the URAL Mountains. Instead I share with Maltby the news that Susan Stamberg's husband claimed to have found two mistakes in the lyrics. Maltby beats me to the punch.

OLSHER. In saying that an Afghani nomad is a Kurd—

MALTBY. It's not really Afghani. It's an Iraqi. There are Kurds in Afghanistan, and I suppose you could get away with it.

OLSHER [*stating the painfully obvious*]. Primarily they're in Iraq.

MALTBY [*with a facial expression that seems to communicate, "Yes, we've all been following the news since 1991"*]. It's where Kurdistan is. I don't know where I got "fistula" from, because I have never seen the word.

[In saying it, Maltby pronounces it fis-TU-la.]

OLSHER. But isn't it actually pronounced FIS-tu-la?

MALTBY. FIS-tu-la.

OLSHER. But the way it scans in your song is fis-TU-la.

MALTBY. Well, yeah. Because there's no reason for it to be right.

Given that the character is a know-it-all, I would have thought there is every reason in the world to have it right. Instead of getting into an argument, I change the subject.

OLSHER. Do you have a community of friends who do puzzles and games together?

MALTBY. No, not at all. I have one friend of my wife's who comes from a Scrabble family. They've played Scrabble every night after dinner for thirty-five years. I can't imagine how dull that would be. She's not a lot of fun to play with, because she knows all those two-letter words. Please. I just find that game not interesting. I resisted doing sudoku for a long time and just sort of fell off the wagon.

OLSHER. You're doing them now?

MALTBY. I do. If you find you've made a mistake, then you throw it away. It becomes irritating and you don't want to do it again.

OLSHER. There's nothing at stake.

MALTBY. If you made a mistake in the crossword puzzle, you'd fix it and put the right letter in.

OLSHER. To me, sudoku is like solitary confinement. I love the crossword puzzle because it creates all these associations and I feel connected to a bigger world of the mind. Sudoku just takes me to this solitary cell that has no connection to the outside world and I feel very claustrophobic in there.

MALTBY. I periodically will go on obsessions. When FreeCell came into my life, I would stay up until six o'clock in the morning doing FreeCell.

OLSHER. What is that?

MALTBY. It's a sort of solitaire game. I had an addiction to FreeCell. There's a game called Spider Solitaire, and I had an addiction to that. I just get these things in my head for a while, and they just completely control me until I finally move on to some other kind of thing.

Before our interview ends, Maltby goes to the next room to pull out some cryptic clues he's just written, starting with "Deserving more, it is our letters that need rewriting" for MERITORIOUS. Readers who send in a correctly completed puzzle are eligible to win a subscription to Harper's.

MALTBY. I have no idea how many submissions I get. I do know that the winners are from all over the place. You know, Tennessee, places you wouldn't imagine anybody would be smart enough or interested enough to do those. They in no way pay for the amount of time it takes to do them. I have a person who tests the puzzles for me. He's just as pretentious as I am, and I like that. He'll say, "Does that really *mean* that?"

Clueless

Francis has had his own share of video-game obsessions.

"Obsessions that come, and they're the thing you do for two weeks, and then you're done. Like when I was playing Zuma." And then, in a stage whisper, "Oh, I was playing too much Zuma."

What's Zuma?

Francis called the game up on his computer. "You're this frog, in an ancient temple, that shoots colored marbles!"

To my mind they look like shattering Christmas ornaments and, somewhat frighteningly, a little too much like Tetris, to which I lost a year of my life. There was no way to recognize the Tetris Year as the mood disorder that it was, since Nintendo is a closed universe with no checks and balances. It was my obsessive music-listening habits that tipped me off: first, Richard and Linda Thompson; then, a few years later, Mahler's *Kindertotenlieder*, the most perfect soundtrack for depression. Seeing concern in the faces of others who witnessed me in these listening marathons alerted me to the possibility that something was wrong.

Crosswords, like Tetris, are dangerous because they are pursued in private, like the eating habits of a binge eater. We are ill-equipped to eliminate obsessive activities on our own. I would argue it's almost impossible. By their very nature, they (video games, rigorous iTunes maintenance, crosswords) trick you into thinking they're helping you, like the alcoholic who reaches for the bottle believing it contains salvation when in fact just the opposite is true.

Now I'm looking for a social obsession. I consider the fact that Will Shortz spends six nights a week playing table tennis. On the surface it appears crazy, and yet, as crazy goes, it seems healthier than sitting alone and filling in empty boxes. Shortz might become a Ping-Pong champion. Even if there were a chance that I might win at the American Crossword Puzzle Tournament—not in the A, B, or C, but in the lowly D division, where I am ranked in the top ten—I can't imagine how doing so would make the world a better place. The most logical endeavor for channeling these obsessive energies is music. For a while, I made part of my living performing folk music for dances and in coffeehouses in Chapel Hill, then quit, because the pressure to earn money took the fun out of it. Now the thought of an *amateur* musical career—in other words, doing it out of love—makes me think I might kill even more than two birds with the same stone.

The Five Obstructions: Ways to Make Easy Crosswords More Challenging

1. On Mondays, Richard Maltby will do the across clues in order followed by the down clues in order, with no jumping around the grid permitted.
2. Maltby has solved crosswords entirely in his head, without writing anything down.
3. I have tried both of these strategies and find they turn the puzzle into a chore. Instead, I make a rule that I must enter 1-Across and then may add only words that cross other words already entered in the grid.
4. Ben Bradlee, former editor of the *Washington Post,* has on occasion solved the daily *New York Times* puzzle as if it were a diagramless, without using the grid as published. "I've been known to show off like that, yeah," he told me. "That's not as hard as it sounds, since they're of a predeter-

mined size." It is hard to imagine how a devotee of crosswords could allow his own newspaper to print a puzzle of no distinction year after year. "I had so much else on my plate, I couldn't get to that."

5. "Another thing you can do is not look at the acrosses," Francis said. "Only solve the downs. I think that's a little more fun. There is a sense in which down clues are harder just in that we're not as used to reading that way. Sometimes if I'm stuck on a down clue I will write out the blanks horizontally because sometimes I'll see the word more easily."

If It's the Last Thing We Ever Do

Everything I know about the world I learned from crossword puzzles. "Old name for Tokyo?" EDO. "South African language group?" BANTU.

And so the idea of a crossword cruise seemed a perfect fit. Etymology alone provided enough justification to book a trip, as "cruise" is thought to derive from a Dutch word for "cross." In a more fundamental way, though, crosswords and cruises share an essential quality: both are highly orchestrated activities designed to create a manipulated, predictable facsimile of the world, free of unpleasantness.

"Nothing bad ever happens in my puzzles!" Thus spake Stanley Newman, editor of *Newsday*'s crossword and author of one hundred puzzle books devoid of references to political controversy, death, and physical or mental illness. For ten days Newman served as crossword guru for a tiny subpopulation of the otherwise theme-less cruise ship, Holland America's *ms Zaandam*, making stops in the Bahamas, Aruba, Curaçao, Costa Rica, and, birthplace of everyone's favorite palindrome, the Panama Canal.

I partook with my friend Electra, a member of the National Puzzlers' League who shares my fondness for cryptic crosswords. Electra is the type of person who, when encountering the phrase *banana plantation*, checks imme-diately to see if it would make a suitable theme answer for a daily crossword. (It wouldn't, as the maximum is fifteen letters.) We were on the lookout for these, as Newman's syllabus culminated in the collaborative construction of a puzzle, preferably cruise-themed, that he would publish in *Newsday*.

Newman has a devoted following. Nine of the guests enrolled in his crossword program were repeat custom-ers, yet his syllabus seemed geared toward beginning solvers. We competed against one another in crosswords and related games, and several hours were devoted to instruction on various topics, including how to solve dia-gramless crosswords. Occasionally, Newman would take questions. A request for techniques in how to improve one's speed in competition yielded the following tips: "Look for a clue you are absolutely sure of the answer for, because erasing takes time," "It's always easier to be sure if one or more letters are filled in," and, "You need to keep an eye on the letter arrangements that are form-ing. Four-letter words that end in K-N? There are not too many."

Indeed, there are none.

Sessions covered such noncrossword territory as sudoku and also lateral-thinking puzzles, which I knew as a child during those long car rides with my father as Minute Mysteries. As Newman explained, to solve lateral-thinking puzzles you must abandon some preconceived notion that turns out to be erroneous. Example: A man rode into town on Friday, stayed three nights, and left on Friday. How was this possible? The man's horse was named Friday.

"The ability to seek out nontraditional solutions has a great benefit in real life." By way of example, Newman told a story about the 2004 World Puzzle Championships held in Croatia. He and his fellow attendees had been served a lavish breakfast and lunch that included free beverages; at dinner, however, their hosts charged for drinks. How to avoid paying without being thought an "agitator" or "subversive?" Newman and his fellow lateral thinkers noticed that fresh fruit was available at the buffet, which they squeezed into glasses. They also melted the ice it was served on, and voilà, juice and water, free of charge.

Electra and I would have benefited greatly had we taken instruction from Newman before signing up for the cruise, since lateral-thinking puzzles try to "throw you off with words that have unexpected meanings." I am still replaying the conversation with Michael Beresky from Special Events Cruises, the trip organizer, and wondering what hidden definition might exist for the phrase *everything included*, since we needed to be cost conscious (which was reflected in our cabin choice, the least expensive at $1,685, already high by cruise standards and certainly by ours). Before long I began to wonder if *everything included* might be a contranym—a word or phrase, such as *cleave* or *oversight*, that has two opposite meanings. As it turned out, everything *cost extra*, both big (excursions in port) and small: DVD rentals, soft drinks, and the occasional latte, necessitated by the brown water served in place of coffee. (It did occur to me that while I had heard veteran cruisegoers rave about the quantity of food available on ships, no one ever seems to praise its quality.)

And so the rest of the cruise became in itself a kind of puzzle. Our challenge: to enjoy ourselves without doubling the cost of the trip. The final tally added an additional 50 percent. (By some twisted logic, this seemed like a victory, especially after it inspired what might have been the perfect cruise-related theme clue—"Exclamation in Talking Heads song"—until I realized that MYGOD-WHATHAVEIDONE is three letters too long).

I also had to abandon my preconceived notion of what would constitute a "crossword cruise." As this was my maiden sea voyage, I may have had slightly grand expectations, envisioning days and nights on a floating planet of like-minded puzzle fiends, complete with impromptu midnight word games of our own invention. It was not to be. In the roughly 213 hours that elapsed between boarding and disembarkation, 17 were scheduled for crossword activities. On days spent at sea, sailing between ports, there were four hours given over to crossword activities. Not taking into account our early dismissal for conflicting shipwide events—I wonder how many of the crossworders were tempted to bolt when someone who identified himself only as Ashley Smash came over the loudspeaker and reminded all on board not only about Bingo but also about the Watch and Brand Name Seminar—7.98 percent of our time was actually devoted to crosswords. Calling it a crossword cruise really seemed like a stretch, considering that the *Zaandam* holds 1,440 passengers and 17 signed up for the puzzle program. That means 1.18 percent of us were there for crosswords. Forgive the math. It's what puzzlers do.

It did seem a little odd that even though there were so few of us, we were not all seated together at dinner. This was sad for Electra and me, because dinnertime is when you really get to know one another. Sitting elsewhere did, however, give us the opportunity to observe that the non-crosswording travelers were equally attentive to nuances of language. I think in particular of the guest at the next table who, when he learned that the man serving him coffee was named Tri, asked if he had a brother named Four. Ha ha ha ha ha!

I immediately started crafting another possible theme entry for our collaborative puzzle: "Most famous line from Sartre's *No Exit.*" (Alas, the answer—HELLISOTHER-PEOPLE—turned out to be two letters too long.)

Once it became clear that this cruise would do little to feed our hunger for crosswords, we knew we needed to change strategy. Our best chance for happiness was to get off the ship. This posed challenges of its own, because (1) ship-organized excursions were *muy caro*, (2) the crew reminds you at every opportunity that if you do venture off on your own unofficial excursion and something prevents you from returning to the ship before it has already set sail, then too bad for you, and (3) so little time is spent in port that unless you do organize an excursion of your own, you're stuck wandering around a shopping zone. Quite a conundrum, but, as logic puzzles go, this one was infinitely more interesting than sudoku.

Our first stop was in the Bahamas, on an island owned and operated by the cruise company. Workers got off the ship and offered massages and sold drinks and beachwear in little cabins by the beach. If we were going to break away from the ship-engineered facsimile of the world, it wasn't going to happen here.

We docked next in Aruba, a land rich in crosswordese, on the very day that the *New York Times* puzzle included ORINOCO, the river basin in South America from which the local ARAWAK people were thought to originate. The shopping was plentiful. We found a patch of green by the ocean and Electra offered how much nicer New York's parks would be if they were populated by IGUANAS rather than squirrels and pigeons.

Next stop, Willemstad, Curaçao, home to the oldest Jewish congregation in North America. Electra and I toured the synagogue, with its sand-covered floor, and the adjoining museum chronicling more than four hundred years of Jewish life in the region—fascinating, yet utterly useless for solving crosswords. And while the chance to shop at the Mr. Tablecloth store was irresistible, what excited us most was the overly large and deformed-looking cinnamon that we bought at the floating produce market and smuggled back home.

It was at that moment, when we least expected it, that we were hit with a dose of reality, and it was glorious. Perhaps because I know about the world largely through crossword puzzles, I tend to think of places as ideas. GDANSK was always "Birthplace of Solidarity"—until I went there and discovered that it is first and foremost a shipyard, and that the people who work there are more interested in talking about exceeding production quotas than they are in Lech Walesa. As for the Panama Canal, my mind always tended toward Teddy Roosevelt and *Arsenic and Old Lace*. That was until I actually witnessed with my own eyes the miraculous system of locks capable of lifting a 60,906-ton cruise ship high into the sky—85 feet above sea level!—using only power generated by water pressure. Words could never capture the thrill of this engineering feat, so I will simply say that if you ever have the chance to travel through the canal, do so.

Since this was the palindrome-producing Panama Canal, at this point we should have turned back to Curaçao, Aruba, and the Bahamas, in that order. Instead, we were dropped in the Panamanian port of Colón, where we ventured beyond the shopping mall that girds the dock and straight into a neighborhood too dangerous for loitering.

That did it. At this point, Electra and I understood that if we wanted to enjoy our final shore leave, in Puerto Limón, Costa Rica, then we would have to organize something. We had a choice: spend hundreds of dollars for a ship-organized excursion, or else venture out on our own for a fraction of the cost. And so, despite repeated warnings about the dire consequences of possibly getting left behind, we hired our own guide, a fellow with a pencil-thin beard sporting seven rings on each hand and a gold dollar sign the size of a potato hanging around his neck, and whose shirt pocket announced his name as Tom Cruise, even though he introduced himself as John. We couldn't have asked for a better real-world antidote to our imprisonment of the previous week. For our benefit he climbed a cacao tree, broke open a pod on the sidewalk, and showed us how to suck the sweet milky substance from the bitter seed, which he bit open to reveal a purple interior. He bought us pipas (similar to coconuts, but smaller) from a roadside vendor, who pulled two from a freezer, hacked off the ends with a machete, and stuck in straws so that we could drink the sweet juice. John promised it would cleanse our kidneys, and I had little reason to doubt him. Or to believe him, for that matter. He drove us to a nature park in the rain forest and, en route, pulled over so that we could take pictures of ourselves holding a three-toed sloth, which was so, well, slothful, it gave off a creepy aura of sickness. All this while John's own toes were still recovering from the night before, when they got a little too close to the metal fan at his bedside and had their tips sliced off. This explained his limp.

It was a desperately needed break from manufactured reality, from crosswords, and from the English language, for that matter. Relying on Spanish that had gotten rusty since college, I missed some of what John said. I can say with certainty that as he drove us back to the ship, I heard him call it the *Zaandam Hussein*, and that if we didn't make it in time, we could stay with him in his house.

Hmm. How about "Last six words of James Joyce's *Ulysses*."

ISAIDYESIWILLYES. Only one letter too long.

Newman handed out the first competition puzzles, promising prizes to those who solved them fastest and with the fewest errors. As he did so, I sensed the glimmerings of a forgotten sensation deep in my chest. What was this feeling?

"Begin!"

Oh, right. That. It's the real reason why I'm an antisocial puzzler in the first place. Puzzles and word games bring out a relentless competitive side that I have spent years trying to tamp down. At one point in the 1980s, I had to give up Trivial Pursuit; it was the full moon, and I was the Wolf Man.

Had I been a proper gentleman, I would have taken my lead from Lon Chaney Jr. and asked to be locked up in a prison cell aboard ship until the competition was over, but that seemed redundant. Instead, at the risk of unleashing the beast, I went ahead and started solving, planning to devour anyone who stood in my way.

And yet.

Although it still pains me to admit this, mine was not the first hand to go up. Who was that speed solver behind me? The short hairs at the back of my neck started to rise. I turned around and looked at the soft-spoken woman who worked for the American Egg Board. She was a return-ing Newman devotee, and she seemed unused to credible competition on these cruises. Perhaps that's why she was staring daggers at me.

Welcome, fellow traveler.

At this point, things could have gone in one of two directions: I could either chill out and embrace the cruise spirit, or else continue pursuing my competitive ways.

And so of course I tore into the next challenge as if I hadn't eaten the entire winter. Sure, behaving this way wouldn't make me any friends, but I wasn't ever going to see these people again.

Our task was to come up with the most eight-letter words using the letters in ORANJESTADARUBA. A special prize would go to the first team to find the near-homophones. Electra had READOUTS and REDOUBTS by lunchtime.

As the afternoon sudoku lecture began, I urged her to show her results to Newman. After all, there were prizes at stake! Electra was raised properly and is thus conscious of appearances. Not wanting to seem aggressively competitive, she resisted my efforts. I therefore had no choice but to grab her answers and hand them in myself. I did take care to give her full credit for the solution, but this had the opposite effect of the one I intended. I dared not look at Electra for fear of daggers from her, as I had thus given everyone the opportunity to hate not only me but her as well.

Finally, the time came for our group to construct a puzzle, for publication in *Newsday*. It wasn't competitiveness but just pure excitement over the pleasure of creation that drove me to throw myself into it with gusto. In fact, I can point to the very moment when I was hooked. As I stared at __ U __ __ __ __ W __ __ , a problematic array of letters and spaces waiting to be filled in (without the aid of computers), suddenly an elegant solution came to me, and it was as if I had given birth to that word. SUNFLOWER!

▨ It's a Small World After All

Even if Stanley Newman were not in the benighted camp that believes cryptic crosswords will never take off in America, still he would never publish the puzzle Francis was making. Lots of bad things were happening, including mental breakdowns of various sorts, a weight disorder. There's incarceration, inebriation, urination. It is surprising that there's no sex, given that Francis wrote an entire book of "adult" crosswords, but drugs and rock and roll do appear. The puzzle contains clues and answers you wouldn't find in a conventional crossword, yet nothing unfamiliar to the readers of this book; in fact, many of the elements will be startlingly recognizable. Despite previous statements to the contrary by Francis, his puzzle is dedicated to the belief that crosswords need not be an escape; as Mahler said about the symphony, crosswords should be like the world itself and embrace everything. Crosswords are part of life, not something separate. Why should they not reflect its totality?

Before we go any further, here are two more cryptic clue types.

6. Anagrams. Ximenes describes himself as "particularly fussy about these." For one, they tend to be overused and he urges restraint. Also, he insists, "they should not be indirect anagrams, which only give a synonym of the anagram instead of the anagram itself." In other words, he's saying it is unfair to make the solver come up with a synonym of the word in the clue and then scramble it; we should only have to rearrange the letters that appear on the page. From Theresa Cunningham's Guide to Solving Cryptic Crosswords: "Grant, a noted eccentric (6)." An "eccentric" treatment of the words *a noted* makes DONATE.

7. Hidden. Here, the answer is hiding in plain sight among two or more words in the clue. From Ximenes himself: "'Give power to some of the policemen—a blessing [6].' ENABLE." Look again. *Give power to* is the definition. "Some of" tells you the word is hidden in the next series of words: *policem*ENABLE*ssing*.

Bouncing Around the Prison System

Stanley Newman passed around one of his *Newsday* puzzles for us to solve. If he had said nothing about the constructor's biography, the answers TRAP and NARC would probably have passed by without notice. They were invested with special meaning when Newman mentioned that the puzzle was made by "an incarcerated individual." His name was Roger.

When I picked Roger up near his rooming house in Sarasota, Florida, the first thing he did was hand me a small white circle the size of a nickel that he had cut from a piece of paper. On it he had written the letters TUIT. Something blocked me from getting the trick, even though I have driven hundreds of times past a restaurant in upstate New York called "Round Tuit."

I met Roger—a lean, bald man wearing glasses with thick lenses that magnified the appearance of being cross-eyed—days before his seventy-first birthday and months after his most recent release. At that point he had spent about half of the previous forty years in prison. I offered to take him to lunch at the place of his choice. He said he liked Long John Silver's. He called for directions on his new cell phone and got the listing for a franchise ten miles away. Using cell phones was still new to him. At first he was going to complain, because he didn't want a recorded message. He was used to speaking to a live person.

I started driving, and within minutes, he had gone from telling me about his childhood in Lewiston, Maine, to his collaboration with a woman who helped him get his puzzles published while he was in prison. I asked why he was incarcerated in the first place.

"Oh, I was afraid you were going to ask that." His collaborator had asked him the same question. "I told her, and she said she wished she hadn't asked. If I say I'd rather not talk about it, then you're going to think something bad anyway. So I figure what the heck."

He let out an especially long sigh and continued: "But, um, I'm more comfortable with myself anyway. I've got the monkey off my back. I had a pretty heavy monkey on my back for a lot of years. It's never been clinically discussed—I've never discussed it with any psychologist, psychiatrist, or anything like that. The background of it, anyway.

"I was, I believe—my *own* diagnosis—retarded in some way. There's been a lot of things that have happened in my life. Take for instance when I was six years old, I lived in the city, in Lewiston. Lived right across the street from a city park, and they had a pool over there, and I used to go over to the pool every day. And every time I left the house—it was right across the street—my mother would say, 'Look both ways before you cross the street.' So I'd go out, stand at the curb, look both ways, and run right into a car. I'd run out and run into a car. I never had a car run into me, thank God. But I'd run into a car! I did what my mother said, look both ways before I crossed the street, but she didn't tell me what to look for! I mean, when you were six years old, and your mother said, 'Look both ways before you cross the street,' you would probably look to see if there were any cars coming, right? So there had to be something missing up here, a screw loose. That's why I say I was somehow retarded. And that had some bearing on what I got into."

Roger did not come across as retarded. Extremely literal minded, yes.

"When I was ten years old I had been getting into bits

and pieces of trouble with the police." Roger pronounced it PO-lease. "Well, we didn't call them the police back then. With the cops. Stealing things, you know. My parents had split up. My mom was still living in the city, my dad lived up in Hartland. And they decided I'd be better off up there. Living in the city was bad for me. And I moved up there with my dad, then we moved in with a family on the farm. And there was already four boys at the farm, and their family, and there was a farm next door that had five girls. And some of the ages pretty well matched. And there was a lot of pairing off, you know, and sex games out in the barn, you know, and I got into that. In fact the two youngest girls, which were a year or two younger than I was, introduced me to it. When that started I was about thirteen, I think, something like that.

"And then later on when I got married, I was in the army. I was overseas. At first there was a trigger to it, I think. There was an apartment next door, and I didn't think anything of it. There was no air-conditioning. This was back in nineteen sixty, in the summertime, and we had the windows open, to get air. I had taken a shower, and I was drying off, and I heard some young girls giggling. I looked around, and there was a window outside the bathroom, and there was this window there, and I looked across the courtyard, and there was a couple of girls. One was our landlord's daughter and the other was her girlfriend who lived over there. And they were looking into my bathroom watching me dry off. They seemed to be, you know, pretty pleased with the situation, and it kind of gave me a rush. So, I don't know, within a day or two I started exposing myself to them 'accidentally'—you know, accidentally on purpose. Not being overt about it.

But that led to being overt, and I exposed myself to other kids, and I wound up being a real active sex offender. I wound up getting kicked out of the service for it. And that carried on when I got back to the States, and I wound up in and out of psychiatric hospitals and mental hospitals and prison."

I asked Roger about the treatment he received.

"It's mostly group therapy. And it's a lot of hype about it, but it doesn't really work. Let's see. Make a left here."

We should have found the Long John Silver's by this point, but somehow our directions did not match up with reality. Roger gave me suggestions for how to find it, and I continued to drive back and forth over the same stretch of highway looking for the address.

"I had prostate cancer a few years ago, and actually I had a radical prostatectomy in ninety-seven, and radiation therapy after that, and that killed my libido. Even the deviant—*thank God!*—tendencies, proclivities, whatever you call it.

"My exhibitionism, I kind of equate to the type of exhibitionism that entertainers experience. They're exhibitionists in a sense. I've heard that some entertainers, while they're putting on a show, they actually become sexually aroused. The sexual offenses that I've committed, I don't recall any that had anything to do with sex itself. I never got aroused, never got an erection while I was exposing myself. It was part of being immature. It was proving, 'Hey, I'm a man. I've got a penis. I'm a man!' I had very low self-esteem, low sense of masculinity. I felt I was entertaining the children. I lost that with my prostatectomy in ninety-seven."

Eventually I realized that the shuttered building set

back from the highway had the same architectural features Long John Silver's used. The restaurant was closed and the building was for sale. When Roger realized we would not be eating where he wanted, he affected a whiny voice.

"I still want my Long John Silver's!"

Our driving episode lasted one hour and six minutes, at which point we finally left the car and headed to Roger's second choice: the buffet at Golden Corral.

"The first time I made some puzzles was the result of one of my sex offenses in Florida. I was up in the Panhandle, Chattahoochee State Hospital. I had picked up typing skills. They had a kind of weekly newsletter at the hospital. So I started making puzzles for that as well as being a typist on the staff. I bought myself a legal pad and pencil and I started drawing grids on that and just filling in words, just to be keeping my mind active. I'd do it on my breaks, when I didn't have anything else to do. I haven't been making any lately. The crossword puzzle business went downhill for a few years, with people spending more time on the Internet. I don't know, I've kind of lost interest in the puzzle. In making them, anyway. I just don't feel like making them."

I wondered if Roger's main motivation to make puzzles was his incarceration, but he thought instead it was because he had become addicted to sudoku. I told him my line about sudoku as solitary confinement. He not only didn't find it funny, he didn't seem to understand it.

"One of the male nurses or something saw that I was interested in sudokus, and he was, too, so he made copies of about two dozen puzzles for me. I do them lightly in pencil and then erase them out and I'm still doing the same two dozen. One of them got torn, so I've got twenty-three. Every night, I get books from the library, I read a chapter in the book, I do a puzzle. I finish the puzzle, erase it all out, stick it on the bottom of the stack, take the top one out, read another chapter of the book, and do the same puzzle over and over and over again. Weird."

Find and Replace *Poetry* with *Crossword*

> Poetry is not a turning loose of emotion, but an escape from emotion; it is not the expression of personality, but an escape from personality. But, of course, only those who have personality and emotions know what it means to want to escape from these things.
>
> —T. S. Eliot

I Am a Chimera

We credit Arthur Wynne with inventing the crossword puzzle in December of 1913. But did he? As it happens, Will Shortz has found about twenty protocrosswords from the preceding decade that were very much like Wynne's word-cross. One puzzle, published in the September 1904 issue of a magazine called the *People's Home Journal*, was exactly the same, with multiple words crossing one another. This puzzle lacked one crucial element, however: a grid. Solvers had to imagine the spaces and fill them in mentally.

Shortz conducted a survey he published in *Games* magazine. Did people consider this a crossword or not? Six out of ten said yes. Shortz was in the minority. He didn't think it qualified, for two reasons. The first is that it didn't lead to more puzzles. While we can trace a direct lineage from Wynne's word-cross to the puzzles that appear in our newspaper every day, this predecessor was an evolutionary dead end. The second is the absence of a grid, which Shortz thinks is no superficial matter. As he likes to repeat, the attraction of the crossword as we know it is that people like to fill in empty spaces.

What seemed maddeningly simplistic at first now has the ring of truth; however, the way Shortz expresses it, in my view, needs some tweaking. It's not that we want to fill in the blanks, it's that we want to immerse ourselves in something big. Something that engulfs us. Something that brings on what Freud described as the "oceanic feeling."

People used to attend orchestra concerts in pursuit of this feeling. Then cinema came along and did the job even better and for less money. And then came theme parks, which Disney describes as immersive experiences. And now video games.

We want to get inside things—crosswords, music, lovers. It's hard for us to think outside the box because we really want to be inside the box.

Falling into Plato's Cave

Meeting radio personalities is usually a terrible idea. They exist most vividly in the listener's head. Real-life encounters disappoint.

Usually, when I am on the receiving end, the comment goes something like this: "Oh, I always imagined you to be older." Or "taller." I suspect these are euphemisms for "more handsome."

On those occasions when I met the people behind the voices that made me want to be on the radio in the first place, there's been some kind of diminishment. I always imagined them to be less awkward.

Joe Frank, on the other hand, was as suave and in command in person as he is on the air. The first time I introduced myself to him, he began the conversation by saying that most people are afraid to meet him because they expect the dark, disturbing persona he affects on the air. "See," he said. "I'm really not so bad."

In fact, he was downright warm and fuzzy. I was the bad guy. I told him that I didn't want to risk damging his powerful presence in my head, and that these encounters always turn out poorly, and that I admired him tremendously. And then I shook his hand and walked away.

I wish I could redo that one—the moment I turned Joe Frank into JOEFRANK.

As Electra and I sailed the Caribbean, crossword constructors back home rejoiced at the possibility that Samuel ALITO would make it onto the Supreme Court. Their excitement was apolitical: his name presents a desirable distribution of vowels.

I began to wonder how thin the line is between the apolitical and the amoral. My mind was still in Poland—

not Gdansk but a small town in the far opposite end of the country. Every day, people board buses headed for Oświęcim. It does not jolt the locals the way it does a first-time visitor, translating it to the name we commonly use for this place: Auschwitz.

You can sit in the room where Zyklon-B was used for the first time. You can enter the showers. The spot that brought home the reality of what happened here was the staircase in the main administrative building. The steps were worn by years of boots treading on them. My shoes sank into the same depressions started by Himmler and Goebbels.

Auschwitz has become shorthand for the most horrible idea of the twentieth century. It is benign when we turn Gdansk and the Panama Canal into ideas. But when you consider that Poles post letters every day to Oświęcim, it makes it harder to let Auschwitz fade into abstraction. It is that same kind of abstract thinking that allows cultured people to stop seeing others as actual humans and to begin reading them, instead, as emblems of problems that must be rooted out of society. If Roger thought of those children as beings with feelings of their own, would he have spent such a huge chunk of his life in prison? It's dangerous to dwell in humanity's Platonic essence rather than in each person's unique, problematic, complicated individualness.

At the Crossroads

I am fed up with the crossword. Even worse, it fills me with loathing. Still, it tempts me in silly ways.

At my last visit to the American Crossword Puzzle Tournament, I ranked much higher than I did during my previous outing. My raw score was roughly the same, but since there were two hundred more people competing, I suddenly jumped from the middle of the pack into the top third. I became flooded with adrenaline when I thought there was a chance I might win the D Division. D Division! I forgot, during those deluded minutes that seemed to stretch the whole afternoon, that I am trying my hardest not to be a competitive person. In fact I even envisioned myself training hard so that I might come back the following year and actually clinch the— yes, the *D Division* trophy. Could I really have taken this seriously? Does anyone in his right mind set such a goal?

I sensed the old beast welling up inside. Francis noticed my agitated state and tried to bring me back to myself. At least to the self I want to become: the person who boasts about being uninterested in crosswords as a competitive sport.

"You have to keep not caring," he said.

You don't need an fMRI to know that crosswords are dangerously addictive. Or that, in large doses, they are depression's ideal diet.

Hitchcock was right. No emotion. Just the illusion of it.

Sure, there are worse obsessions. The bad things we put into our eyes can't damage us as much as the things we put into our mouths, noses, and arms. But addiction, finally, keeps us from living fully. It numbs us, and for someone who has devoted his life to appreciating the aesthetic, it is hypocritical to wallow in the anesthetic. Given my family history, it might be smarter to spend less time chasing dopamine. As coping mechanisms go, this one has run its course.

Crosswords could never satisfy in the way I had hoped. I was asking too much of them.

Mojo

Through a twist of fate, the core group of our Doma Breakfast Club—JoAnne, Bill, and I—moved and ended up within a two-block radius. Our new coffee place, Mojo, is not stuffed with celebrities. On one Saturday morning the three of us showed up at the same time for an impromptu minireunion. I was struggling with the *Times* crossword and passed the puzzle over to JoAnne. This had almost never gone well in the past. JoAnne, who normally does just fine with the crossword on her own, is one of the people in my life whose natural confidence with the puzzle is diminished by the aggressive crossword pheromones I seem to emit. But something was different this time. Instead of passing it back and claiming an inability to keep up, she examined it closely and soon enough put a word in. Soon Bill was contributing answers, and before long, the puzzle was filled in. It felt as if I had done nothing to bring this moment about. It happened on its own, and I savor it. I have reconciled myself to the likelihood it might be quite a while before it happens again, but that's okay. At least I know it's possible.

◼ Almost There

I've come to the conclusion that watching someone make a crossword puzzle is like watching someone stare at a computer screen. It's not only that I slowed things down by staring over Francis's shoulder for six hours. My presence forced the process (or much of it, anyway) to take place in an unnaturally continuous work session.

"How long would you typically go at a single stretch?" I asked.

"Not that long!"

I started to pack up my things.

"It depends," Francis continued, "if you sort of get into a really focused state. And it's easier to lose track of time when you're just doing a grid. I'm more likely to do short bursts on cluing, and then do something else, and then come back to it."

That's how Francis finished making the puzzle—in the nooks and crannies of his daily life. As he wrote clues during the days that followed, he sent them to me by e-mail. He explained how he arrived at each one and issued a semiapology for one clue: "'Dogs pee a lot' is sort of juvenile . . . but I cannot deny that it makes me laugh. And it's so nice and concise! (And undeniably true.)"

Here are two more categories of cryptic clues, as outlined by Ximenes.

8. Improvised Clues. By lumping together a number of clue types under this rubric, Ximenes makes it seem as if they appear only occasionally. In fact, some are quite common. Here are three examples.

The possibilities are theoretically endless; this is just to give you a sense of them.

    a. Heads and tails. As a cryptic indicator for ULULATE, Ximenes conceived a "South African beheaded not long ago" (Z-ulu, late).

    b. Alternating letters. This one, from the *New Yorker:* "'Eight botch theft after ignoring the odds (5).' The answer, 'OCTET,' is a group of eight, and can be gotten by ignoring the odd letters of bOtCh ThEfT.'"

    c. First or last letter only. Sondheim squeezed an entire movie script out of this type of clue: the plot of *The Last of Sheila* turns on the realization that the last letter of "Sheila" is A.

9. &lit. This one comes to us from the Guide to Cryptics at crypticsmonthly.com: "The trickiest type of clue to write, the &lit. clue is not in two parts, as are all the other clues we have discussed . . . . '&lit.' is an abbreviation for ' . . . and literally,' since you read the clue in its entirety once to get the wordplay and once again literally to get the straight definition. For example, the clue 'It can get you routed a different way! (6)' gives you DETOUR. The wordplay says that DETOUR can get you the letters in 'routed' put a different way; notice that thus the wordplay uses every word in the clue. Then, read literally, 'It can get you routed a different

way!' is a fair straight definition for DETOUR. Traditionally, in North America, &lit. clues have been signaled by an exclamation point, in what is a kind of gift to solvers (letting them know what kind of clue it is before they start to solve it). In the past few years, however, as solvers have become more sophisticated, some constructors have stopped using the exclamation point as a signal, either using, instead, a question mark—which might just as well indicate a punny clue—or no mark at all."

You're almost ready to try a cryptic crossword on your own. Remember that words can be reversed by going "back," for example, in both across and down clues, but only in a down clue do reversals go "upward" and the like.

Keep in mind also that clue writers have one especially devious trick at their disposal: they often repunctuate to serve the surface meaning of the clue in a way that does not serve the "grammar" of the cryptic meaning. You may argue that this is unfair. You may be right. Nevertheless, this is how the tradition took hold over the twentieth century and there's not much I can do about it.

The good news is, you'll remember, that there can be no extraneous words. Every single element of the clue has to be either a definition or part of the cryptic instruction. This means that even if you don't know the straightforward, definitional answer, everything you need to decode the answer is staring you in the face.

If I have managed to pique your interest in the ways crosswords have something to say about the larger world we live in, that will be fine. If I have succeeded in getting you to try just one cryptic crossword, then I will be ecstatic.

Here, let me make it easy for you. (See the next page, please.)

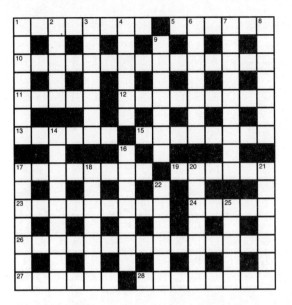

ACROSS

1. Discussed drugs: a shabby kind of reward (8)
5. Eccentric bosses' haunt (6)
10. For Doctor House, a new organizing technique? (5,3,2,5)
11. Celebrities and I disembarking from flight (5)
12. Commercial way of speaking is something that it's hard to stop doing (9)
13. Stymies state officials (6)
15. I met Dean getting smashed, resulting in severe loss of mental capacity (8)
17. Time in rehab destroyed source of inspiration (3,5)
19. Quietly retracted private denial in pen (6)
23. They're working on a crossword clue between the sheets: "Roman god personifying the Sun" (9)
24. Oddly, darker aims concealing a lofty ambition (5)
26. Review of esoterica, as in a nonstop stream of words (4,11)
27. For example, a person paying rent (6)
28. Escort Isolde around something that makes the heart beat faster (8)

DOWN

1. Nods, reading through verse's words reflectively (7)
2. Shrew's home and beatnik's home under attack, initially (5)
3. Increases the price of feast after damage by kitchen, to start with (5,2)
4. Not for or against "Time Out of Mind" (6)
6. Vehicle is destroyed by Cecil (7)
7. Came back with uncovered pies, eating last two of Wheat Thins dramatically (9)
8. Foster girl from southern United States meeting actress Paquin (7)
9. Dogs pee a lot (7)
14. Independent in disorganized U.S. Senate is least comfortable (9)
16. Seaside riots: an unpleasant subject to see in a crossword (7)
17. Polite performance aboard German Air while ascending (7)
18. Cathartic moment found in relative comfort (7)
20. Awesome! One insect is glowing (7)
21. So-called leaders of new order may invade Norway and Luxembourg (7)
22. Hear Ike breaking and entering? So crazy (6)
25. Improves a book with trims, moving the excellent part to the front (5)

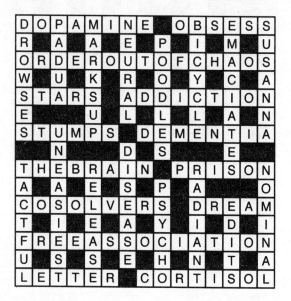

ACROSS

1. Discussed drugs: a shabby kind of reward (8)—"Discussed" should set off your homophone alert. In this case, the "pun" applies to more than just the one word that follows. "Dope" and "mean" are alternative words for *drugs* and *shabby*. They are separated by the letter *A*. DOPAMINE is a *kind of reward*.

5. Eccentric bosses' haunt (6)—If you spell *bosses* "eccentrically," you get OBSESS, which is one meaning of *haunt*.

10. For Doctor House, a new organizing technique? (5,3,2,5)—Another anagram here: the "new" take on *For Doctor House, a* is ORDEROUTOFCHAOS, which is Stephen Sondheim's technique for *organizing* his world. If that feels like something of a stretch to you, the question mark is Francis's way of saying he hears you.

11. Celebrities and I disembarking from flight (5)—When the letter *I* is "disembarking" from STAIRS (another word for *flight*), you're left with *celebrities*, or STARS.

12.   Commercial way of speaking is something that it's hard to stop doing (9)—Let's play Concentration! A *commercial*, or AD, is followed by a *way of speaking*, or DICTION. Put them together and you have *something that it's hard to stop doing*.

13.   Stymies state officials (6)—The abbreviation for *state* is ST. Baseball *officials* are UMPS. Together, they spell out a synonym for *stymies*.

15.   I met Dean getting smashed, resulting in severe loss of mental capacity (8)—When the letters in *I met Dean* are "getting smashed," they are rearranged, "resulting in" DEMENTIA.

17.   Time in rehab destroyed source of inspiration (3,5)—*Time*, represented by the letter T, followed by the letters *in rehab* "destroyed" gives you THE BRAIN.

19.   Quietly retracted private denial in pen (6)—*Quiet* is indicated in musical scores by the letter P. A *denial* by an army *private* is NO SIR, which is then "retracted," or reversed. This wordplay appears "in" PRISON, which is one definition of *pen*.

23.   They're working on a crossword clue between the sheets: "Roman god personifying the Sun" (9)—SOL, the Roman sun god, appears "between" *the sheets*, in other words, slipped into the middle of COVERS. The answer is COSOLVERS.

24.   Oddly, darker aims concealing a lofty ambition (5)—Read *darker aims* "oddly," i.e., read only the odd letters, and you find the word "concealing" DREAM.

26.   Review of esoterica, as in a nonstop stream of words (4,11)— When you "review" or reorder the letters *of esoterica as in*, you get FREE ASSOCIATION.

27.   For example, a person paying rent (6)—An especially devious double definition, best derived by starting at the rear.

One meaning of *person paying rent* is LETTER. That leaves you with *For example, A.* This, for me, is an Ah! Moment.

28. Escort Isolde around something that makes the heart beat faster (8)—This is a hidden clue. The phrase *Escort Isolde* is "around" CORTISOL.

DOWN

1. Nods, reading through verse's words reflectively (7)—DROWSES. This is one of those instances requiring mental repunctuation. "Reading through" is a signal that the answer is hidden. "Reflectively" tells you it goes backward. *Nods* is the definition of DROWSES, whose letters appear backward in *verse's words*.

2. Shrew's home and beatnik's home under attack, initially (5)—It helps to remember your Shakespeare for this one. A *beatnik's home* is a PAD. *Under attack*, "initially," tells you to use just the first letters of those two words, i.e., U and A. That means the definition is PADUA, which is the *shrew's home* in Shakespeare's comedy.

3. Increases the price of feast after damage by kitchen, to start with (5,2)—MARKS UP. *Feast*, or SUP, comes "after" *damage*, or MAR, which is "by" *kitchen*, which "starts with" K.

4. Not for or against "Time Out of Mind" (6)—Take T *(time)* "out" of NEUTRAL *(Not for or against)*, and you have NEURAL, which can be defined as *of mind.*

6. Vehicle is destroyed by Cecil (7)—The letters *by Cecil,* when "destroyed," become BICYCLE.

7. Came back with uncovered pies, eating last two of Wheat Thins dramatically (9)—A real toughie. *Came*, when it comes "back," spells EMAC. When *pies* is "uncovered"— in other words, the top is taken off—you're left with IES, which is "eating" the *last two* letters of *Wheat*. The definition of *thins dramatically* is EMACIATES.

8. Foster girl from southern United States meeting actress Paquin (7)—Another charade: S (*southern*) + US (*United States*) + ANNA (*Paquin*) = SUSANNA (as in, the *girl* from the Stephen *Foster* song).

9. Dogs pee a lot (7)—P + OODLES.

14. Independent in disorganized U.S. Senate is least comfortable (9)—I (*Independent*) is "in" a "disorganized" (i.e., a reordering of the letters in) *U.S. Senate:* UNEASIEST.

16. Seaside riots: an unpleasant subject to see in a crossword (7)—When the letters that make up *seaside* start to "riot," we get DISEASE. (Apologies to Stanley Newman.)

17. Polite performance aboard German Air while ascending (7)—A *performance*, or ACT, is "aboard" (i.e., inserted into) the German word for *air* (LUFT), which, "while ascending" in a down clue, becomes TFUL. The definition of *polite* is TACTFUL.

18. Cathartic moment found in relative comfort (7)— RELEASE. *Relative* can be abbreviated as REL. Another word for *comfort* is EASE.

20. Awesome! One insect is glowing (7)—RAD (*Awesome!*) + I (*One*) + ANT (*insect*) "is" RADIANT.

21. So-called leaders of new order may invade Norway and Luxembourg (7)—The *leaders,* or first letters, of *new order may invade Norway and Luxembourg* are NOMINAL, which is another word for *so-called.*

22. Hear Ike breaking and entering? So crazy (6)—A homophone for *Ike* inserts itself into ("breaking and entering") a homophone for *so,* which is PSYCHO.

25. Improves a book with trims, moving the excellent part to the front (5)—EDITS. By "moving the" E, or *excellent part to the front* of "diets," which is a synonym for *trims,* you get EDITS, the definition of *improves a book.*

From Square One

The critic Walter Pater wrote that all art constantly aspires toward the condition of music. That's true of the radio show I created, and it seems to hold for crosswords as well. And so, after a lifetime of stand-in activities, I woke up to the reality that what I would really like to do is involve myself again with music itself.

I am looking forward to tomorrow, when solving a crossword is no longer mandatory, as research, and becomes something I do because I want to. My new daily activity is practicing the bass clarinet, a departure for me. Until this point I have played instruments such as the piano, one of the most complicated machines in music. I switched to the accordion, thinking it less mechanical mostly because it vibrates so warmly against my chest. Still, when I play, I approach it through my head and have never figured out how to bypass my brain, to play from the heart.

Like a person with Asperger's syndrome who has no instinct for reading the emotions of others, playing music with feeling is, for me, a behavior learned through hard work. But, after a lifetime of singing "If I Only Had a Brain," I now pay closer attention to the Tin Man. The lesson of my deep involvement with crosswords is that I need to stop thinking my emotions and start feeling them. My hunch is that music will get me there in a way that crosswords have not.

I have yearned to play the bass clarinet for many years. Despite my proficiency on other instruments, I could never make a sound on a woodwind. That changed when I walked into a music store in Saratoga Springs, New York, and laid down $400 for a vintage horn. I blew into it and made a sound that was, if not exquisite, at least audible. I continue to practice and get better and have since upgraded to a Selmer Paris, the Rolls-Royce of bass clarinets. As midlife crises go, this one is much cheaper than a fancy car and a lot more gratifying.

Unlike the accordion and piano, which are well suited to solo playing, this instrument cries out for performance in a group. I have found fellowship by joining a wind ensemble at Lehman College in the Bronx. Our programs have their cheesy moments, as the concert band repertoire tends to sound like *Star Wars* no matter what is being played, and there's little chance of Mozart anytime soon. Still, I am grateful to be there, for several reasons. One is that this band represents the only group of people in my New York life that is not segregated. Behind me, in the trumpet section, sits a retired doctor. My fellow bass clarinetist will be the first member of his family to graduate from high school. And the feeling of being inside the music is more satisfying than anything I know. Sitting as one member of a collective and following the lead of an autocratic conductor is an excellent way to lose one's self. This instrument requires control of the breath, which is how we understand the spirit—the mind, as opposed to the brain. Playing it seems more like an extension of living itself.

I think it is a good sign that I am attracted most of all to the bass clarinet's timbre—a step in the right direction, away from dwelling on the abstract relationships between the notes. I love the reedy sound, its range extending down to where I wish my own could reach. It is the voice I almost have.

Acknowledgments

With deepest thanks to:

John Chaneski, Jonathan Crowther, Marcel Danesi, Nick Griffin, Hendrik Hardeman, Helen Kimble, Jed Levine, Mandy Rice, Mike Stutzman, Greg Villepique, and Edwina White for the gift of their time and reflections

Katie Dixon, for pointing me to Mandy

Anna Roberts, for introducing me to Candis, who continues to identify herself as Anna's mom this many years after she led me to the British crossword mafia

Megan Martin and John Snyder, for helping me see into the brain

The Corporation of Yaddo

Marcy Heisler and Paul Lazarus, you know what you did

Danielle Gustafson, Sue Johnson, Brad Klein, Andrew McCarthy, Dolores Rice, Joe Richman, Patti and Jay Rohrlich, and Josh Seftel, who put up with me when I needed to be put up

Jesse Green and Andy Newman, who were there when I needed a rabbi

Fred Plotkin, for sharing more than just an agent with me

Heather Christensen and Taylor Smith, for their taste

Henry Alford, Carmelle Arad, Brittain Ashford, Heather Bourbeau, Robert Boynton, Christine Butler, Erin Cox, Jeremy Denk, Jon Delfin, Leigh Ann Elisio,

Anya Grundmann, Amy Harmon, Maira Kalman, Jill Krauss, Brooke Kroeger, Richard McCann, Rick Meyerowitz, Rick Moody, Richard Panek, Amy Reynaldo, Ellen Ripstein, and Susan Stamberg, just because

To all of you, a great big THANK YOU.

And then there are the people who were absolutely, positively essential to the completion of this book. Extra-special thanks to:

Across

1 Woman who had the idea in the first place is made of starch, graham crackers (5,7)

3 Puzzle guru, wise, without energy, eats llama heads in front of Republican in smoking Jaguar (4,6)

6 Phenomenally generous, perceptive reader who deserves much gratitude and who hates semicolons; endlessly noble in front of German people (8,4)

7 Patient editor is a goose with a growl (5,6)

Down

2 Agent for good! (4,6)

4 Crazy zest, autism, with missing It Girl (4,8)

5 "A thousand, say, billfolds" as heard by *ER* writer (3,8)

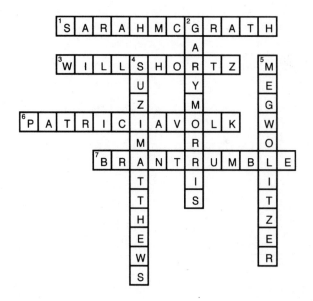

About the Author

DEAN OLSHER has been a broadcaster for more than thirty years, most of which he has spent in public radio. He was an arts and culture correspondent for NPR News as well as the creator and host of *The Next Big Thing*, a popular national show. Currently, he is a visiting professor at NYU's Arthur L. Carter Journalism Institute.